MEDICAID
AND
LONG TERM CARE
HANDBOOK

The Essential Guide to Using Medicaid and Public Benefits to Pay for Nursing Home Care

By Sean W. Scott, Esq.

Masveritas Publishing
4673 Alisa Circle · St. Petersburg · Florida 33703

Library of Congress Cataloging-in-Publication Data

Scott, Sean W., Esq.
Medicaid and long term care handbook : the essential guide to using medicaid and public benefits to pay for nursing home care / by Sean W. Scott.
    p. cm.
Includes index.
Summary: "A resource on the use of Medicaid to pay for the costs associated with a long term stay in a nursing home or assisted living facility. Includes sample strategies to protect assets and qualify for Medicaid benefits"–Provided by publisher.
ISBN 0-9785050-4-2 (pbk.)
1. Nursing homes–Law and legislation–United States. 2. Medicaid–Law and legislation. 3. Older people–Long-term care–Law and legislation–United States. 4. Older people–United States–Finance, Personal. I. Title.
 KF3826.N8S38 2010
 344.7302'2–dc22
                           2010028711

Version 1.0
Printed October 2010

Published by Masveritas Publishing, LLC
4673 Alisa Circle, St. Petersburg, FL 33703
Copyright © 2010 by Sean W. Scott, Esq.

This book is designed as an overview of the law of Medicaid as it relates to the cost of long term care. The laws discussed in this book vary greatly from jurisdiction to jurisdiction and often change. Consult a lawyer familiar with elder law in your state.

The author and publisher have used their best efforts in the writing of this book, but make no representations or warranties as to its accuracy or completeness. They also do not make any warranties implied or otherwise of merchantability or fitness for a particular purpose. Any advice given in this book is not guaranteed or warranted and may not be suitable for every factual situation. Neither the author or Masveritas Publishing shall be liable for any losses suffered by any reader of this book.

For my father, who always wanted to be lawyer.

TABLE OF CONTENTS

• •

Why planning is important.
When to plan.
The three ways to pay for care.
Why protect assets?

Distinguishing Medi*caid* from Medi*care.*
When does each program pay for the nursing home?
The differences between the two programs.
Medicaid and the assisted living facility.

WHO NEEDS TO READ THIS BOOK?

• •

You never thought a nursing home would be part of your life. Then suddenly, it seems the possibility of the nursing home or assisted living facility becomes the reality. How are you going to pay for the care? Are you going to be financially wiped out? What options do you have? This book is designed to provide you with answers to those questions. It is a great starting point to familiarize yourself with the topic of paying for long-term care using the Medicaid program.

Are you or a member of your family thinking about a nursing home or assisted living facility? Is there a progressive, degenerative disease process happening to you or someone you care for? Are you just getting older and worrying about who is going to take care of you? Then you need to read this book NOW.

Where you live and apply for Medicaid benefits changes the Medicaid rules you have to play by. For the sake of clarity, I frequently refer to the specific rules that are applicable in the state of Florida. While Medicaid is generally similar throughout the 50 states, the specifics of its application, including the allowed amounts of income and assets and many other factors, change from state to state. You must localize the information in this book to your particular state.

I cannot stress enough the importance of competent legal advice from a local elder law attorney. Only he or she will be able to adequately assess your situation and apply your state's specific Medicaid rules to qualify you for Medicaid benefits. Still, I have included information tables in the appendix that highlight some of the specific eligibility requirements for all 50 states. This specific information can generally be substituted for the Florida information referenced in the main section of the book.

HOW THIS BOOK IS ORGANIZED

This book is divided into the following chapters:

- INTRODUCTION TO MEDICAID PLANNING – Outlines the concept of long-term care planning. Don't skip this part. Every part builds on the next. Medicaid is a complicated subject that requires a good basic foundation.

- MEDIC WHAT? – Explains the differences between Medicaid and Medicare? It is important not to mix them up.

- ELIGIBILITY REQUIREMENTS – Shows how to determine eligibility for Medicaid benefits, including the criteria and the tests used to qualify for benefits.

- THE BIG CHANGE IN MEDICAID – Medicaid underwent significant changes in 2005-2007. The new Medicaid eligibility rules are game changers and dramatically increase the number of applicants denied benefits.

- TRANSFERRING ASSETS – Discusses why giving assets away is the quickest way to disqualification. You cannot simply transfer assets to become eligible for Medicaid benefits.

- INCOME AND ELIGIBILITY – How does income effect Medicaid eligibility? This chapter shows how to still be eligible even if you are over the income cap and how to move income to a spouse in need.

- ASSET PRESERVATION STRATEGIES – Identifies key factors and techniques used to obtain eligibility. Includes discussions of some commonly employed strategies used to protect assets from the cost of long-term care.

- MEDICAID ESTATE RECOVERY – Explains why you can't leave the problem only half solved. You must address the estate plan of both the applicant and the spouse. Failure to do so may create either disqualification or subject assets to being taken by the state to pay the state back for benefits paid.

• CHOOSING A NURSING HOME – Paying for the nursing home is one problem, but which one are you going to use is another challenge. There are many resources available to help make your selection. By asking some good questions and doing some research you can be closer to finding the right nursing home.

• CONCLUSION – Good news, despite the seemingly impenetrable maze that is Medicaid law and the ever tightening of eligibility requirements there are still options to become eligible for Medicaid benefits.

• APPENDIX – Find your state specific information here. Includes the State of Florida internal memoranda outlining the implementation of the Deficit Reduction Act.

DISCLAIMER

Since your author is an attorney, you would expect some sort of disclaimer to protect from potential legal problems. Here it is: This book is provided for informational purposes only. It is not to be considered or construed as rendering legal advice and it does not constitute a binding legal opinion. The reader should consult with an experienced elder law attorney with expertise in his or her particular state to review his or her specific situation and apply the current law to that situation. Please use this book for what it is intended, an introduction to the laws and issues surrounding nursing home care and Medicaid eligibility.

WAY FINDER ICONS

• •

Throughout the book you will see "way finder" icons that help guide you and further your understanding of the topics being discussed. Each way finder either stresses a key point, helps clarify some particular legal jargon, highlights a real-life example or points out a situation where you need to exercise extra caution. Pay close attention when you see the following:

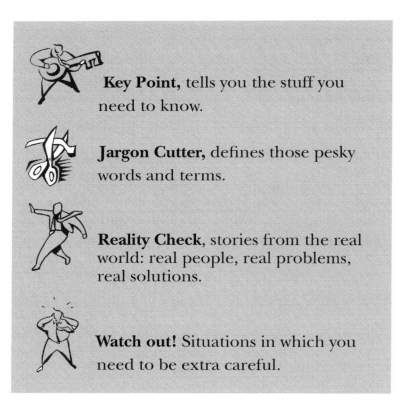

Key Point, tells you the stuff you need to know.

Jargon Cutter, defines those pesky words and terms.

Reality Check, stories from the real world: real people, real problems, real solutions.

Watch out! Situations in which you need to be extra careful.

ABOUT THE AUTHOR

• •

Sean W. Scott, Esq. maintains a practice in both elder law and life care planning in the state of Florida. For the last 20 years he has focused his practice on the legal needs of the senior community with particular attention to Medicaid law, asset protection, incapacity and estate planning. Mr. Scott integrates the law with life care planning principals to best serve the needs of the aging client.

Mr. Scott has written numerous articles on the subject of elder law and is frequently requested as an expert commentator for the media including newspapers, radio, and television. He is a frequent speaker before groups of lawyers, accountants, health care professionals, social workers and the general public. He is also the host of the podcast "Age With Confidence" available on iTunes and on FLMedicaid.com as a free download.

The practice of elder law provides him with the opportunity to assist a segment of our population to avoid the financial ruin that can result from an extended stay in a nursing home. Helping a family in need, at a time when all seems lost by showing them the way to financial security, affords him the kind of personal and professional reward few practice areas can match.

He has been a member of the National Academy of Elder Law
Attorneys since 1991, a member of the Academy of Florida Elder
Law Attorneys and has served on the board of directors for the
Florida Gulf Coast Alzheimer's Association as the organization's
treasurer, the former chair of the Clearwater Bar Elder Law
Committee, and a former director of Neighborly Care Network.

FOREWORD - WHY THIS BOOK, WHY NOW? A FEW THOUGHTS FOR THE READER

The United States Supreme Court accurately described Medicaid as among "the most intricate ... Byzantine" texts "ever drafted by Congress." The renowned Justice Henry Friendly called the Social Security Act "almost unintelligible to the uninitiated" and another famed appellate court famously stated that the statutes and regulations "are among the most completely impenetrable texts within human experience." In this text, Elder Law Attorney Sean W. Scott has succeeded in the impossible by explaining, in plain English, how Medicaid applies to ordinary Americans.

Medicaid is the primary government program covering long-term care for Americans. Without it, many of us, our parents, grandparents and friends would be without care at end of life. Yet in America, our system does not provide long-term care for all. The system only pays for long-term care when a person is down to $2,000 in assets. Because the cost of home care, assisted living and nursing home care is so high, most people cannot afford to pay without becoming impoverished. After "spending down" to the Medicaid poverty limits, these middle-class and upper-middle-class Americans are now solely reliant on the government dole, having no money left to pay for everything the government will not cover. Because money buys care, these people now struggle to maintain quality care and quality of life.

The purpose of this text is to provide a starting point for families to plan for the future and to provide solace and direction for those who come to it at time of crisis. The good news is that there are solutions and Sean W. Scott presents them in this book. Generous with his knowledge, he shares potentially life-changing information with you. In this text, Sean W. Scott takes complicated state and federal rules and laws and explains it in — believe it or not — an easy to understand and even fun format.

Having practiced Elder Law in South Florida for over 20 years, I am well aware of the crisis in which people find themselves when facing long-term care. It seems to come out of nowhere, this freight train of trauma that can blind-side the unprepared. After 50 years of marriage, a wife watches as her husband deteriorates into near-total dependence. Her goal is to keep him at home as long as possible but, she has her own limits whether admitted to or not. A loving daughter attempts to be a caregiver for her parents while juggling her own family and work commitments. She watches as her work and family life suffers but knows that she must deal with the core human issue of her parents needs in their final years. I have met with thousands of people dealing with these or similar issues. I know how important a tool Medicaid can be.

Medicaid is far from a panacea (this book explains that well) but it absolutely saves lives and enhances quality of life.

Your goal is to succeed in aging with dignity and quality of life, both for you and for your loved ones. To be successful in aging, especially "aging-in-place" at home, you must arm yourself with all of the resources and knowledge you can. Many outside forces conspire against your success. The long-term care system is dominated by insurance companies, health care provider groups, care facilities, home care agencies and other providers, all of whom can be very helpful but all of whom are in it to make money. The sad truth is that some of the providers put profits over the interests of their clients/patients, usually unintentionally. In order to succeed in achieving the highest level of care and the highest quality of life, you must become educated in how to work this system. Use this text on Medicaid and long term care as a starting point, always keeping in mind your end-game — to achieve the highest level of care and the highest quality of life.

While this text is an incredible resource that will help you and many others, do not think of it as a substitute to consulting the right professionals. It takes elder law attorneys years to understand how to counsel their clients and guide them through the long-term care maze. Do not make the mistake of thinking that you can do this alone. While it may sound self-serving for me to suggest you consult with an elder law attorney, it is not. You cannot do this alone. You need help.

Pay for it. If you select the right professionals to help you, the money you spend will come back to you many times over.

I am going to close by asking you to do something important. After you have read through this book and learned how to make the Medicaid system work for you, tell at least one other person. The information contained in this book can save tens or hundreds of thousands of dollars but more than money, it represents what that money can buy — quality of care and quality of life. Share this information so you can help others. That is why Sean Scott wrote this book.

Scott M. Solkoff, Esq.
Delray Beach, Florida

CHAPTER **1**
AN INTRODUCTION TO MEDICAID PLANNING

* *

In this chapter:

Why planning is important.
When to plan.
The three ways to pay for care.
Why protect assets?

* *

As we or our loved ones age the possibility of long-term care looms in our consciousness. When the nursing home becomes a fact of life, issues of displacement, the loss of independence, role reversals and in most cases the stark reality of financial ruin are all thrust upon us as part of the nursing home experience. Catastrophe looms large for a family when facing an $8,000 or more per month bill for nursing home care.

Most people think that they will never go to a nursing home. My own father was a great example of this way of thinking. When asked if he was ever going into a nursing home the answer was not just no, but hell no. In retrospect he was right and might be considered one of the lucky ones having died instantly from a heart attack instead of a prolonged stay in a nursing home. According to statistics reported by National Public Radio, one out of every three men will be in a nursing home before they die, for women, it is one out of every two. While you may think you or loved one will never go into a nursing home, more often than not it is a modern reality. It is a reality you should have a plan for.

Key Point. "No agency of the government has any right to complain about the fact that middle-class people confronted with desperate circumstances choose voluntarily to inflict poverty upon themselves when it is the government itself which has established the rule that poverty is a prerequisite to the receipt of government assistance and the defraying of the cost of ruinously expensive, but absolutely essential, medical treatment."

Justice Lawrence Bracken,
Appellate Division of The New York Supreme Court.

When to plan

A failure to plan is a plan to fail. As you age the possibility of nursing home care changes to the probability of nursing home care, and finally at some point to the certainty of a nursing home. The more challenging question for most of my clients is not how to solve the problem of paying for care, but when to solve the problem, when to begin to plan. The techniques and strategies used to preserve assets quickly sort themselves out during the planning process we undertake for each client. What is not so clear though is the right time to plan for the nursing home. Crystal balls are hard to come by. If we all had the magic ability to see into the future and know exactly when we would need nursing home care, then we could all start planning at the perfect time.

I have found that the majority of my clients usually fall into one of three categories when it comes to Medicaid planning: The planner client, the writing on the wall client, and the emergency client. Which one are you?

The planner client is best described as the type of person who knows what his breakfast menu will be three weeks from now. He has it all planned out. He is more than focused on the future, he is fixated on it. He takes great solace and peace of mind with having all the details worked out well in advance.

The writing on the wall client has had some indication that a problem looms ahead. A diagnosis of Alzheimer's or Parkinson's, a succession of small strokes, or a rapid decline in health all indicating that a nursing home stay is likely. Steps should be taken at this time to address the future need for care and the payment of that care.

The last type of client is the emergency client, or the "Uh-oh" client. Uh-oh as in "Uh-oh, my loved one is in the nursing home and I don't know how I am going to pay for it." The good news, though, is that even if someone is in the nursing home it is still not too late to preserve some if not all the person's assets and obtain Medicaid benefits to pay the cost of care.

When planning for a nursing home stay, timing is a significant consideration. The sooner you begin to plan, the more options there are to protect the assets. Many different strategies exist to preserve the assets of the Medicaid applicant. The key is knowing what to do and when to do it. This is one area where the experience of a qualified elder law attorney can be invaluable. He or she can bring to bear years of experience to help in the decision making process to determine when to start planning.

Each one of these three different types of clients has their own unique solutions to the Medicaid qualification problem. As you might imagine though, the more time before the crisis occurs, the more you plan ahead, the more choice of strategies you have and the easier the problem is to solve.

Watch out! Under the DRA 2005, transfers of any amount as a gift will disqualify you from Medicaid benefits. If you want to make gifts or charitable contributions you need to take action to avoid the disqualification trap. With some good legal advice and some simple planning you can still give without the disqualifying effects gifts now make on Medicaid eligibility.

Paying the cost of long-term care has plagued American families for decades. The change in American demographics, the departure from the multi-generational household to a dispersed family, and the advances of medicine that enable all of us to live longer have created a crisis in care for the elderly. We turn more and more often to the services provided by a nursing home or assisted living facility to provide the necessary care. How do you pay for this care? When faced with paying the nursing home or assisted living bill you have three options: private pay, long-term care insurance, and Medicaid.

Private Pay

The first option is to pay from your own resources. We call this the private pay option. Many of my clients have saved all their lives to take care of themselves in their old age. Then one day, suddenly old age catches up with them. They now face the problem of caring for themselves or a loved one in a nursing home or assisted living facility. The saying goes that we save for a rainy day. When the nursing home finally becomes a reality, it's not just raining, it's pouring. There is absolutely nothing wrong with using saved funds to take care of you or your family member, however, in all but the richest families, the cost of care will wipe out all the savings in short order. I often refer to the nursing home situation as a war of attrition. One where you win by going backwards as slowly as possible. In cases where you fail to plan or take action the war is over in short order with you as the loser.

One of the common myths connected with the option of private pay is that you need to pay privately to get the best care. This is just not the case. Private pay patients and Medicaid pay patients receive the same quantity and quality of care. There are actually strict federal rules that require nursing homes to treat both private pay and Medicaid patients equally. If the nursing home discriminates against Medicaid recipients, then the facility can lose its ability to participate in both the Medicaid and Medicare programs. Nowhere in the patient's chart is there an indication of their payment source. The only people who know who is paying the bill are the facility's billing staff.

The other common myth is that before you can qualify for Medicaid benefits you must spend all your assets on your care. Again, not true. While this kind of spend down strategy will obviously get you to Medicaid qualification, it does so at the prohibitively high cost of all your assets. There exist many legal ways to obtain the Medicaid eligibility that do not require you to spend all your funds on care. Read on.

Insurance

The second option used to pay for care is long-term care insurance. Insurance of any kind is a way to manage a risk, whether it be the risk of a fire in your home, or a car accident or going into a nursing home. Insurance is a valid method of managing the risk of a nursing home stay. As with any type of insurance make sure that you have something to insure. If your assets are only modest, spending thousands of dollars a year to protect your relatively small nest egg makes no sense. Long-term care insurance does not manage the risk of going into a nursing home, but instead manages the risk of how to pay for the care without going bankrupt. If you are close to, at or below the requirements for Medicaid eligibility you have no need for the insurance. Similarly, if you are way above the eligibility requirements, say over a million dollars in assets, you are effectively self insured and may be able to manage the risk without using insurance.

Long-term care insurance has positive points but also some big negatives. The most often cited negative of long-term care insurance is its cost. If you ask someone why they have not purchased long-term care insurance the response is almost always, "It is too expensive." Policies for the typical senior can run anywhere from $5,000 to $10,000 or more per person per year. To get a ball park figure on your cost for insurance check out the Federal Employees Long Term Care Insurance Program on the web at *https://www.ltcfeds. com/ltcWeb/do/assessing_your_needs/ratecalc*. Even if you are not a federal employee and eligible for this particular insurance program the web site provides an easy to use rate calculator demonstrating the effect of age and coverage choice on the cost of a typical long-term care policy.

Seniors living on a fixed income who are already worried about tight budgets often do not see the value in long-term care insurance to pay for care at some point in the future when they are trying to figure out how to pay for immediate expenses today.

One of the good things about using long-term care insurance is that it will often pay for more than just the nursing home. Many policies today pay for other types of care, including home care and assisted living care. Long-term care insurance also provides a degree of certainty and peace of mind by solving the problem now instead of relying on a less certain solution in the future.

Key Point. When talking about long-term care it is important to distinguish assisted living and nursing home care. A nursing home provides a higher degree of care and has the ability to meet more significant medical needs of their clients. A nursing home is required to have a Registered Nurse available 24 hours a day. An assisted living facility (ALF) provides only modest assistance with daily living needs and is very limited on the type and scope of medical care it can provide. Historically, Medicaid has not paid for assisted living care. This is changing as states experiment with Medicaid. Florida Medicaid, for example, has introduced the Nursing Home Diversion Program that provides coverage for assisted living care as well as home care in certain circumstances.

If you do purchase long-term care insurance, make sure that you have enough coverage, not only for today's cost of care, but for what such care will cost in the future. One of the most ironic situations I see as an elder law attorney is when a person has insurance but only for a small daily amount. For example, if the policy pays $80 a day and the cost of care is

$200, the $120 a day shortfall presents a significant problem. The person, despite having insurance, despite having paid premiums for years, will still have to use Medicaid to make up the $3,600 per month difference to pay for the care. Talk about adding insult to injury.

If you decide to buy insurance, a good rule of thumb for the amount of coverage you need is the average daily rate, which depending on your location can run from $200 per day to more that $450 per day. Also make sure to select the option for an inflation rider, sometimes called a future purchase option, to help keep up with the increase in the cost of care in the future. The length of coverage should be no less than five years. Also make sure that there is coverage for assisted living and home care, and that there is no prior hospital stay requirement.

Under new rules recently enacted in many states you have the option of participating in something known as the Long-term Care Insurance Partnership Program. These states, including Florida, offer the ability to purchase a particular type of long-term care insurance that effectively lets you keep more assets when you apply for Medicaid. Under these partnership policies you get a dollar for dollar increase in the amount of assets you can keep and still qualify for Medicaid. For example, $100,000 of long-term care coverage equals an increase of $100,000 in additional assets you can keep and still qualify for Medicaid benefits.

Reality Check. A prospective client came into the office with a long-term care insurance policy for his mother who was in a nursing home. On first look it appeared to provide a decent benefit and would significantly defray the cost of care for a period of three years. Upon closer inspection the client had chosen an option when purchasing the policy that required a three day prior hospital stay before the policy would pay any benefits. Why would she have chosen such an option? Cost. That choice lowered her monthly premium, but since she never went to the hospital prior to her entry into the nursing home (she suffered from Alzheimer's disease) she never triggered the coverage and the insurance did not pay.

Medicaid

The third way to pay for care is by using the public benefit program called Medicaid. Medicaid is a jointly funded state and federal program that among many things, pays for nursing home care. It has its origins in the welfare system originally created in 1968 by President Johnson. Medicaid was created along with Medicare to provide medical care for at least some citizens in our country. Both programs are the result of President Johnson's unsuccessful attempt to create a national health care system. Through various lobbying efforts, notably by the American Medical Association, combined with the political environment at the time, he was unable to create a universal health care system. What we ended up with was a split system, one system, that paid medical expenses for the poor, called Medicaid, and one system that paid medical expenses for the elderly, called Medicare. Oddly enough Medicare made no provision for the continuing payment of care in a nursing home. It was left to Medicaid to pay for nursing home care.

Under the original Medicaid program, seniors would impoverish themselves, basically going on welfare to get the care they needed. Spouses would divorce to get access to benefits. Assets would be exhausted and spent down to nothing. Life savings would be wiped out paying for nursing home care until finally the government would step in with some assistance. This "solution" often created more problems and required the person, usually an elderly individual, to reach poverty levels in order to be eligible for help.

Recognizing that perhaps this was not the best way to take care of our aging population, President Reagan changed the federal law in 1986 in order to reduce the burden on our seniors and to keep them from impoverishing themselves.

This metamorphosis in the Medicaid law established new criteria to determine eligibility for public benefits. The new changes increased the amount of assets a person could keep and still be eligible for Medicaid assistance to pay for care, eased restrictions on transfers and implemented new protections for the spouse of the Medicaid applicant. It was at this point that Medicaid effectively changed from a program focused on the poor to much more of a middle class entitlement program more akin to Medicare.

Many people still believe that the Medicaid program is welfare; quite simply it is not. While Medicaid's beginnings come out of a poverty program, nursing home Medicaid has evolved into our country's answer, for good or bad, to the pressing social problem that care in a nursing home presents.

The Medicaid law in 1986 was quite liberal in its application. It allowed people to easily move assets to qualify for benefits. Since then there have been repeated changes in the law to limit and reduce access to Medicaid. There has been a steady swing of the legislative pendulum toward more and more restrictive rules designed to disqualify more and more people from accessing Medicaid benefits. The greatest swing recently took place under President Bush's leadership with the enactment of the changes to Medicaid contained within new federal legislation referred to as the Deficit Reduction Act of 2005. These draconian changes were meant to all but kill off Medicaid. Every state has adopted the new rules, but as with

many things Medicaid related each state has implemented
the new legislation in different ways with different effects on
Medicaid eligibility.

The combined changes over time have created the
convoluted legal structure that we use to determine eligibility
for Medicaid benefits. Qualifying for benefits is not as easy
as "Let's see your bank statement, okay, you're under the
limits... you get benefits." Instead, there are look-back periods
of three and five years, income caps and income trusts to get
around these caps, transfer penalties and waiting periods,
disqualifying transfers, exempt transfers, good trusts and bad
trusts, different rules for spouses and single applicants, even
an asset is not an asset; it is either countable or not countable
depending on individual circumstances. For those of you
familiar with the nonsensical story of Alice in Wonderland,
when dealing with Medicaid, you have gone down the rabbit
hole and nothing is ever as it seems.

Long-term nursing home care is expensive, averaging from
$6,000 to $8,000 per month in Florida to more than $14,000
in other regions of the country, specifically the Northeast.
More often than not, the family does not have sufficient
income to pay for the ongoing cost of care and goes into a
negative cash flow situation. This means that there is more
going out then is coming in. There is a steady and rapid
depletion of the family's assets as they are used up to pay for

the cost of care. The loss of assets is further accelerated and compounded if there is a spouse in the picture who is also trying to maintain a life outside the nursing home. When the other spouse is still trying to survive at home, he or she has to maintain the home, pay everyday expenses, as well as pay the added expense of the nursing home.

The rapid drain on the family's resources produces a bleak outcome: Complete depletion of assets, insufficient income to maintain the spouse still at home, and little or no inheritance to pass on to the children.

Why protect assets?

Why make an effort to preserve the assets of the nursing home resident? I believe that there is nothing inherently wrong with depleting all the assets on nursing home care until the assets are gone. We save for that rainy day and when the nursing home shows up in our life it not just raining but it's pouring. I do believe in options though and that there are three compelling reasons why you might want to take action to avoid sending everything to the nursing home.

The first reason to protect assets is to make sure that sufficient assets are maintained to take care of the spouse who is not in the nursing home. Husband and wife have usually combined their efforts throughout the marriage to create a pool of resources that they both can draw upon to support them as they age. When they run into the issue of long-term care, suddenly these resources start disappearing into the nursing home leaving the healthier spouse without sufficient funds to meet his or her needs.

The second reason to plan is to preserve some form of legacy for the children. You may have seen the bumper sticker that states, "I am spending my grandchildren's inheritance." Rarely though is this sentiment true. An informal poll of my clients reveals the number one reason for saving their money is "...to give it to the kids." I can't tell you the number of times that a son or daughter of a client protests that they do not want mom or dad's money. They miss the point. Whether they want the money or not is not relevant. What is relevant is what mom or dad would want. Many times I am dealing with the adult child of the medicaid applicant and ask him or her what would their parent say if he or she were sitting at my conference table? Would they want you to spend all their money on the nursing home if you had an option not to?

The third, and most overlooked reason, is to preserve the assets for the benefit of the person who is in the nursing home. By taking action to preserve the assets of the nursing home resident you can then use those preserved funds to augment and supplement the care the person is receiving in the nursing home. Those preserved funds can be used to pay for a private room instead of a shared room. The preserved funds can be used to pay for additional therapies, transportation or entertainment. Those funds can be used to pay for family members to fly in from distant cities to visit the resident. One of my favorite uses for the preserved funds is to pay for private duty nursing care to come in and provide one-on-one care for a few hours a day. All of these additional things benefit the resident and greatly improve their quality of life. None of them could be paid for without preserving the resident's assets.

It is my hope that this book will help you begin the process of understanding the issues surrounding planning for long-term care in a nursing home. These are serious issues. Occasionally, we may feel overwhelmed because there seems to be no way to avoid these problems. Let me assure you that nothing is insurmountable. It is also my intention that after reading these pages you will be less overwhelmed by the crisis the nursing home can present. There are solutions to this seemingly unsolvable problem. With good planning and assistance no one needs to be wiped out by the costs of long-term care.

CHAPTER 2
MEDIC WHAT?

● ●

In this section:

Distinguishing Medi*caid* from Medi*care*.
When does each program pay for the nursing home?
The differences between the two programs.
Medicaid and the assisted living facility.

● ●

Medicaid vs. Medicare

Medicaid and Medicare sound similar, look similar on the page and do similar things. However, Medicaid is not Medicare. Medic "AID" differs significantly from Medi "CARE", but because of the similarity of the spelling and pronunciation, many people confuse the two programs.

Most of us are familiar with the Medicare program. Either we or our parents have used it to pay for medical care. We have all seen the deduction on our paychecks or social security payments. This deduction is basically a premium payment for Medicare. Medicare is a type of public health insurance that pays for health care for people over 65. (Medicare also covers people receiving social security disability payments regardless of age.) It will pay for, among other things, hospital and doctor visits. Every person who has made sufficient payments into the Medicare system during his or her working years is eligible for Medicare after turning 65.

There are three core "parts" to Medicare: Part A, Part B and Part D (drug benefits). The "A" part pays for hospital visits and charges, while the "B" part picks up a portion of your outpatient doctor visits and certain other medically-related services. One thing Medicare does not pay for is long-term care in a nursing home, right? Here is where it gets confusing. Part "A" will sometimes pay for a short stay in a nursing home for rehabilitative purposes after a qualifying three-day stay in a hospital. Medicare will pay for nursing home care under these circumstances, but even then, it does so for only a limited time of no more than 100 days and only for so long as the patient is improving in their condition and needs rehabilitative services.

Watch out! Medicare does not guarantee a full 100 days of coverage in a nursing home. Medicare may terminate coverage at any time if the patient stops progressing toward recovery. If the patient stops getting better or plateaus in his or her recovery, Medicare ends. It is not uncommon for Medicare to terminate early, suddenly requiring the patient to start paying out-of-pocket for the nursing care.

Unlike Medicare, most of us have never encountered the Medicaid program. Medicaid is often referred to as a "needs based" program. Its eligibility requirements are based on the perceived need for assistance as determined by the individual's financial and medical situation. You must meet these eligibility requirements before the Medicaid program will help pay for care.

Further in this book are more detailed explanations of the specifics needed to qualify for Medicaid as well as how to meet those requirements.

Nursing home care is part of our overall health delivery system in the United States. Hospitals, physicians, therapists, and nursing homes form a web of care that is our society's method for providing health care. Medicaid fills the gap left open by the Medicare system's failure to adequately cover nursing home care by paying after Medicare ends its coverage.

Medicaid and Medicare are two different benefits programs, each with its own set of rules and coverages. Together they provide a somewhat integrated solution to the problem of paying for long-term care. Medicare focuses primarily on the short term, skilled, rehabilitative part of the problem and Medicaid provides an extended, custodial long-term care solution when Medicare terminates its coverage.

The following chart summarizes and compares Medicaid and

Medicare.

Medicare	Medicaid
• Health insurance for seniors.	• Needs-based health program.
• Pays for no more than 100 days of nursing home care.	• Pays for long-term care.
	• Pays for medications.
• Requires Part D to pay for medications outside the hospital.	• Individual must meet income and asset limits to be eligible.
• Must have contributed to Medicare system to be eligible.	• Individual must be over 65, disabled or blind.
• Pays for hospital care and related medically necessary services.	• Requires mandatory contribution of ALL recipient's income.
• Must be over 65 or disabled to be eligible.	• Individual state-by-state differences create a different program in each state. (Generally similar, but may be different in specific application.)
• May have a co-pay provision depending on the services received.	
• Federally controlled, uniform application across the country.	

A comparison of the Medicare and Medicaid programs.

Generally, Medicare is a stop gap solution that provides a bit of breathing room to assess the needs of the person in the nursing home. Either the person is getting better and going home or they will stay in the nursing home. Note, that Medicare will not pay anything towards a stay in an assisted living facility.

> Key Point. Medicare has a maximum period of coverage equal to 100 days. Once the patient uses up that coverage Medicare ends. To reset Medicare coverage, the patient must be out of the nursing home and hospital for at least 60 days or have been in the nursing home for more than 60 days without receiving "skilled" services. The person must, however, have another 3-day qualifying stay in the hospital to restart coverage.

Medicaid is really the only long-term solution to pay for nursing home care. Even though the Medicaid program has strict income and asset limits, there are strategies that can be used to restructure the applicant's financial situation to qualify for Medicaid benefits. By adjusting his or her finances, a person can preserve all of the assets to augment his or her care, take care of the well spouse, or preserve the assets for other family members.

Medicaid and assisted living facilities

Historically, Medicaid only paid the cost of the nursing home. There was little or no financial assistance for assisted living care or home care. The reason for this is that assisted living was traditionally equated by the government with a housing issue and not a medical issue. Over time, however, many assisted living facilities added more assistance for the resident, increased the level of care they provide to almost the level of a nursing home. The end result is that the assisted living facilities are taking care of sicker people, longer.

States are experimenting with alternatives to traditional Medicaid to help defray the cost associated with nursing home placement. Some states have been implementing pilot programs to pay for care other than nursing home care. These programs are often referred to as "waiver" programs because the federal government waives compliance with certain federal Medicaid rules. In Florida, for example, a Medicaid waiver program called the Nursing Home Long-Term Care Diversion Program was created to help delay placement in a nursing home by taking care of the person at home or in an assisted living facility. Check to see if your state has a waiver program to help with the cost of assisted living care. Contact information can be found in the appendix at the back of this book.

The Florida Nursing Home Long-Term Care Diversion Program is an example of a Medicaid program designed for seniors who need extra assistance in order to remain at home or to live in an assisted living facility. This program, started in October 2003, provides a wide range of services to make it easier for seniors to get the care they need, to live in the community, and stay out of the nursing home. As part of the Medicaid program it has almost identical qualification requirements.

In order to be eligible:

- You must be 65 years of age or older
- You must have Medicare Parts A & B
- Your income and assets must meet the levels required to be in a nursing home under Medicaid. (Steps can be taken to meet the requirements with the help of an elder law attorney.)
- You must be medically/clinically eligible meaning that you require some help or supervision with 5 activities of daily living (ADL) such as bathing, dressing, walking, toileting, eating, transferring, or;
- Require some help with 4 ADL plus require supervision of medications, or;
- Require some help with 3 ADL and have a diagnosis of Alzheimer's Disease, or;
- Require total help with 2 ADL, or;
- Have a diagnosis of a degenerative or chronic condition requiring daily nursing services
- You must be determined by the Florida Department of Elder Affairs to be a person who can be safely taken care of at home or in an assisted living facility, in lieu of nursing home placement. (The program is NOT designed to provide 24-hour care in the home.)

The Diversion program acts much like a managed health care plan or HMO. The goal is to provide a one stop shopping experience where all the needs of the client can be met through one source. A key component of the program are care management companies known as qualified providers. These providers direct, manage and control the services and care being provided to the client/patient. They deal with each client on a case-by-case basis and manage the care of the client so as to keep him or her from going to the nursing home.

The range and scope of services provided by the Nursing Home Diversion Program are impressive and can include:

- Short term respite care
- Prescription drugs
- Assisted Living services
- In home assistance with bathing, dressing, and personal activities
- Help with household chores
- Adult day care
- Coordination of medical care
- 24/7 nurse line for medical questions
- Durable Medical equipment
- Consumable medical supplies including incontinence supplies
- Nutrition assessment and planning
- Home-delivered meals and nutritional supplements
- Escort to medical appointments
- Home adaptation services, (ramps, bath bars, etc.)
- Payment of Medicare deductible and co-insurance.

Reality Check. One of the first clients that my office helped qualify for the Diversion program is a great example of what can be done with these waiver programs. In this particular case the wife was taking care of her aging husband. The husband had severe dementia as well as significant complications from a massive stroke. The wife was doing all she could to keep him home but his needs were rapidly outstripping her abilities. After slightly adjusting the couple's finances to meet Medicaid's requirements, the law office brought in a qualified provider to supply care management and home health care services, all paid for by Medicaid. Because of the Diversion program and qualified provider's involvement, the husband remains at home today.

The Diversion program differs from traditional nursing home Medicaid in two very significant ways. First, when using Medicaid to pay the costs of nursing home care there is essentially a guaranteed acceptance onto the program assuming you meet the technical requirements for eligibility. Second, the vast majority of nursing homes accept Medicaid as a payment source, meaning you have your choice of facilities. The Diversion program is not as widespread as nursing home Medicaid. Unlike nursing home Medicaid which is funded by both the federal and state government, the Diversion program is state funded only and is subject to political pressures and state legislative budgets. It has demonstrated a propensity to run out of funding in the middle of the fiscal year resulting in a freeze on the program's services and future enrollment. Additionally, not all assisted living facilities participate in the program resulting in limited choice of facilities.

The Diversion program has great promise to be an added benefit. In most cases it provides an opportunity to provide care in a less restrictive setting than the nursing home. The Diversion program, however, is far from a perfect solution. Many of our clients find the Diversion program frustrating because of the difficulty getting selected to participate in the program and locating a participating facility. Still it is a better solution than no solution at all and should always be considered when planning for care.

The Diversion program, as with many other Medicaid waiver programs, suffers from one major problem, lack of funding. These programs routinely run out of money and stop taking new participants. These programs rely on the state's budget for funding. There are finite amounts of money available. Once the amount of budgeted money is reached the programs will typically freeze taking on any new participants. Typically, the only way to get on to one of these frozen programs is through attrition. Basically, as one participant leaves the program for some reason, another can come on to the program. In some states such as Florida, there have been some legislative attempts to find creative funding to help move people to less restrictive, and less costly ways of providing care. An example of such a program is called Transitional Medicaid. This program takes the funding that would have been used to pay for the person in a nursing home and uses it for the cost of care in an assisted living facility. In order to qualify for this particular Florida program you must be moving from the nursing home to the assisted living facility after a stay of at least 60 days and being approved for Medicaid benefits.

An alternative to Medicaid we that we have been looking at more and more to help pay assisted living expenses is a Veteran's benefit called Aid and Attendance. If you are a Veteran and have served during war time, you may be able to qualify for Aid and Attendance. This program has its own set of unique eligibility requirements, some less restrictive than Medicaid, and some more restrictive. When counseling a client we often look to see if they can be eligible for both programs.

CHAPTER **3**
MEDICAID ELIGIBILITY REQUIREMENTS

●●

In this chapter:

How to determine eligibility.

The importance of assets and income.

The different rules for married and single applicants.

●●

The Eligibility Requirements

In order to qualify for Medicaid, the applicant must meet the Medicaid program's requirements for eligibility. The specific requirements the applicant must meet include: (1) basic medical need referred to as a level of care; (2) age or disability; and (3) the financial situation of the applicant including the applicant's income and assets. In order to be eligible for Medicaid, the applicant must satisfy all three requirements.

First Requirement – Medical Need

This is the "Are you sick enough?" requirement. Medicaid requires that the applicant be unable to care for himself or herself without substantial assistance. What degree of care or level of care is substantial enough? The person must have an impairment or illness severe enough to limit his or her activities of daily living to a point where a nursing home is the only appropriate placement.

The specific standards used to determine if the medical need is present are:

- The person's needs must require twenty-four hour nursing care in a "skilled care facility." A skilled care facility is one where professional nursing services such as physicians, respiratory therapists, audiologists, physical and occupational therapists are available;

- The person's needs are so medically complex that he or she requires supervision, assessment or planning by a registered nurse;

- The person must need the care on a daily basis;

- The person needs ongoing involvement of a registered nurse or other professional in the individual's medical evaluation and the implementation of a treatment plan;

- The person needs continuous observation in order to monitor for complications or changes in the status of his or her condition; and

- The care the person needs should not be of a degree which would normally be provided by a hospital.

This first requirement is generally one of those things that you know when you see it. By the time I see my clients the medical need requirement is usually a foregone conclusion and easily met. Generally, people do not try to place their loved one in the nursing home any sooner than they absolutely must. Typically, we find that by the time placement is actually made, the caregiver has waited well past the point when they should have made the decision.

Although in some situations, particularly when the person is suffering from a form of progressive disease like Alzheimer's, the need for nursing home care can sneak up on the family. The slow progression of the disease over time can make it difficult to know when to make the move to the nursing home.

Second Requirement – Aged, Disabled or Blind

In order to be eligible for benefits the applicant must be either over 65, be characterized as disabled, or blind. Disabled is defined as the inability to perform gainful activity for a period of time that is expected to exceed one year. For example, a 60 year-old with Alzheimer's would satisfy this requirement if the Alzheimer's disease sufficiently impairs his or her ability to work to such a degree that he or she is qualified as disabled. (Note that the person need not actually be declared disabled by the Social Security Administration or be receiving Social Security Disability payments.) A 70 year-old, on the other hand, clearly meets the age requirement and need not be disabled as long as he or she has the medical need and passes the financial requirements.

The general rule here is that the person needs to be 65 years old or older, however the exception to this rule allowing disabled individuals under 65 to qualify makes this a particularly easy requirement to meet.

Third Requirement – Financial

The third and final requirement is the one in which most people are interested. It can also be the most confusing requirement due to the number of variables that must be considered, and the special rules concerning moving assets and income. The financial requirement is further divided into two parts: The assets of the applicant and, in some states, the applicant's income.

The states are divided into two major camps. About half of the states consider the applicant's income to establish eligibility, known as income cap states, and the others known as medically needy states use income merely to determine the amount of the state's contribution. Florida is an income cap state. (Some other income cap states include Arizona, Arkansas, Colorado, Iowa, Louisiana, Oklahoma, Oregon, and Texas.) To help you identify the particular requirements in your state see the appendix in the back of this book.

Watch out! Extreme caution is advised if using this book for states other than Florida. You must consult with an elder law attorney in your state to assess the laws particular to your jurisdiction. See the appendix for more state specific information.

We will address each aspect of the financial requirements next, starting with assets and then income.

Asset Levels – 50 Percent States, 100 Percent States and Married versus Single

To determine the exact amount of assets that the applicant may keep, we first have to know whether the applicant is married or single. The change in the Medicaid laws in 1986 had the effect of increasing the number of seniors who could qualify for the Medicaid program. Congress was especially concerned with making sure that the spouse of the nursing home resident would not be forced into poverty.

There is a division among the states when it comes to how to treat assets. We call some states 50/50 states and others 100 percent states. The difference between the two is in how the states calculate the amount of assets the spouse of the married applicant can keep. In some states the spouse is limited to 50 percent of the combined assets up to the maximum community spouse resource allowance. Michigan is an example of a 50/50 state. In 100 percent states the spouse can keep up to 100 percent of the community spouse resource allowance. Florida for example is a 100 percent state.

Jargon Cutter. The term for the spouse who is not in the nursing home is "community spouse." This status is important since the community spouse is afforded special considerations. If both spouses are in the nursing home there is no community spouse and you must treat each spouse as a single applicant and use the asset limit for a single applicant.

The amount of assets allowed for eligibility is quite different depending on whether we are talking about an applicant who is married or one who is single. A Florida married couple in 2010 may keep up to $111,560 in countable assets. ($109,560 for the community spouse resource allowance combined and $2,000 of assets for the applicant spouse.) A single person, including widows, can only have $2,000 in countable assets. (The $2,000 limit increases to $5,000 if the income of the applicant is under $808 per month.) It is important to update these eligibility requirements on an annual basis as they change every year. Please visit our web site at www.virtuallawoffice.com to get the most up-to-date eligibility information. The following chart summarizes the eligibility levels for assets and income in Florida:

Allowed Assets (Florida)*	Applicant	Community Spouse	Allowed Monthly Income
Single	$2,000**	n/a	$2,022
Married	$2,000**	$109,560	$2,022 for the applicant spouse.

* See the appendix for your state's numbers.

** Asset limit is increased to $5,000 for applicants with income *less* than $808 per month.

Income and asset eligibility requirements in Florida.

What's an Asset?

Assets are broken down into two categories, countable and non-countable. Some assets are counted, some are not when determining eligibility. This is an important distinction. Many applicants have assets that are non-countable and therefore do not negatively impact eligibility for Medicaid. For example, the first $500,000 of the value of the primary residence is not counted. The total value of the home of the Medicaid applicant, prior to 2006, was not counted as an asset. However, legislation signed by President Bush in February 2006 limits the protection for the home to the first $500,000 in value. The excess value will now be counted as an asset, potentially disqualifying the applicant. It is important to note that states have the option to increase the cap to $750,000 for the home's value.

What happens to the home after the Medicaid beneficiary dies is a separate issue. See the section later in the book on Medicaid Estate recovery for more discussion on the home's status after the death of the Medicaid beneficiary and how it may be at risk of loss to the state.

It is so discouraging for me to hear clients say that they have sold their home in a last ditch effort to generate cash to continue paying for nursing home care. Why did they do such a rash thing? Because they did not know any better. Such ignorance of the law can cost your family dearly. I must stress that the primary residence is not counted as an asset. Exclude it (subject to the new $500,000 limitation) from your total assets when calculating eligibility. There are other types of non-countable assets, the car and a burial account, but none as significant as the home.

Be careful when determining which assets to count. Often, clients erroneously believe that a joint bank account is only treated as half an asset. This is not so, 100 percent of the asset is counted. Do not think that the other person on the account, your son for example, can withdraw the bulk of the account and put it into his name, the law also specifically forbids this. Any transfer from a joint account is treated as if the applicant made the transfer thereby disqualifying the applicant.

Some assets, such as those you may have forgotten or don't always associate with something that you actually own, can put you over the asset cap. A common example is that little life insurance policy you have been paying on for years. It probably has built up quite a nice cash value which will be counted as an asset. Life insurance cash value is counted if the total face value of all policies exceed a certain amount. ($2,500 in Florida, different in other states. See Appendix E) How about your pre-paid burial plan? If it is not irrevocable it will be counted as an asset. It is particularly bad to find out about these surprise assets at the time of the Medicaid application when you are staring over the table at the Medicaid official. Surprise assets such as IRAs and burial contracts are counted if steps have not been taken to change them to non-countable assets. The asset level requirement is not as easy as it would seem.

Watch out! Assets discovered after being approved for Medicaid can destroy eligibility. In one of our cases a life insurance policy was discovered by the son after we had qualified the father for Medicaid. Several months had gone by when a policy notice was sent from the insurance company to the father's home. The son had no idea the asset existed until this notice arrived and therefore it was not disclosed during the application process.

Once the asset was discovered and disclosed to Medicaid, the beneficiary was disqualified from benefits. To make matters worse he now owed Medicaid for the payments Medicaid made for his care. Eventually the matter was resolved and the client went back on Medicaid. He did lose the insurance policy though. The moral of this story, make sure you know where all the assets are.

Income Level

About half of the states do not consider the income of the applicant when determining eligibility for Medicaid benefits. The states that do consider income are called income cap states. Florida is one of the income cap states. In addition to looking at asset levels, Florida imposes an additional factor to consider when determining eligibility; the income of the applicant. To see how your state handles income see the appendix in the back of this book.

In Florida, the 2010 income limit is set at a maximum of $2,022 per month. This cap amount is based on the applicant's gross income, not his or her net income. This means that a deduction such as the Medicare premium and any withholding tax must be added back to determine the applicant's gross income. In income cap states, an applicant who is over the cap, even by a dollar, is not eligible for benefits. We will see though, that this problem has a solution later in the book. Again the income limit changes on an annual basis. Be sure to get updated information at our website www. virtuallawoffice.com.

Having too much income disqualifies the applicant who is over the cap even though he or she may have no other assets and no other means to generate additional cash flow. While the applicant may have a relatively high income, he or she may not be close to the amount required for care which often averages $6,000 per month. The applicant has fallen into what we call the Medicaid gap, too much income to qualify for benefits, too little income to pay for care. What can be done in this situation? Are you out of luck? Do you need to move to a state that doesn't look at income? There is a better solution.

Just as important as determining what is an asset, is identifying what is considered income. At the risk of oversimplification, every source of income is considered countable income. Social Security, pensions, disability, VA benefits, interest income, non-taxable income, IRA distributions, annuity income (regardless of whether it is taken out of the annuity or not), dividends, and everything else that the applicant receives is considered income. Do not fall into the trap of counting only taxable income. Whether taxed or not, Medicaid still considers it income.

Watch out! In an example of irony, those people that have long-term care insurance may also need to apply for Medicaid benefits due to insufficient coverage. The payments from the long-term care insurance policy are usually counted as income and can push the applicant over the income cap.

Prior to 1993, if the applicant was over the income limit there were few, if any options, for the person to fix this problem. Sometimes the nursing home would provide services at a reduced rate; sometimes they would not. Many times the person would have to change to a less than desirable nursing home or move to a non-income cap state. In 1993, though, Congress again modified the laws regarding the Medicaid program, and while they took away many planning opportunities, which further restricted the ability to preserve assets, they gave people who were over the income cap a solution to avoid the Medicaid gap. The solution is called the qualified income trust. The income trust is described more completely in a following section.

When a person is on Medicaid, his or her income is used to help pay for the care in the nursing facility. In order to qualify for and maintain eligibility for benefits, the applicant must pay for part of his or her care on an ongoing basis. This payment is called the patient responsibility. The patient responsibility helps offset the state's costs in providing care.

Calculating the amount of patient responsibility is simple. The applicant contributes all of his or her income to the nursing facility minus a small personal needs allowance. (See the appendix for your state's amount.) If there is a community spouse, then he or she may be able to keep a portion of the applicant's income based on his or her need. This is called the spousal diversion or minimum monthly maintenance income allowance. The exact amount due the community spouse is calculated based on a formula. Generally, the community spouse can divert enough of the applicant's income to raise his or her income, in the year 2010, to $1,822 per month. If the spouse has significant expenses related to housing including rent, mortgage payments, property taxes, and insurance then he or she may be able to divert more income from the applicant up to a total income of $2,739 per month. The amount changes from state to state, be sure to check the appendix to see your particular state's information and to get updated amounts at our web site.

The patient responsibility also includes amounts that are being deposited into an income trust. This income must be paid to the nursing home as part of the patient's responsibility each and every month. By whatever route, all of the patient's income, except for a few small deductions for personal needs or a spousal diversion, must go to the nursing home.

CHAPTER 4
THE BIG CHANGE IN MEDICAID

● ●

In this chapter:

The Deficit Reduction Act and you.

Changes to transfer penalty rules.

Increasing the look-back period.

Why Annuities are bad for planning.

DRA and the home.

● ●

Why the Deficit Reduction Act of 2005 is important to you.

If you are applying for Medicaid benefits to pay the nursing home be prepared for the Deficit Reduction Act of 2005 to impact your eligibility. Recent changes to Medicaid have made becoming eligible much more difficult. In late 2005 the Senate and House of Representatives approved sweeping "reforms" that restricted seniors' access to benefits used to pay for long-term nursing care. The vote was close with the House voting 216 to 214 in favor and the Senate tied 50 - 50 requiring the Vice President to cast the deciding vote. This new legislation referred to as the Deficit Reduction Act of 2005 or DRA 2005, was a fundamental and sweeping change to the Medicaid program. The language of this new law effectively disqualifies nearly every applicant for Medicaid nursing home benefits by changing the eligibility requirements. If your brain just paused and went "Huh?" Let me repeat: Because of this new legislation, nearly every nursing home resident who applies for Medicaid benefits should be disqualified.

From time to time Congress changes the eligibility rules for Medicaid benefits. Since 1993 the law has been relatively stable. But in 2006 it was as if the pendulum of change that had been stuck broke free and ushered in new rules regarding eligibility that imposed perhaps the most draconian eligibility standards yet seen. I have included an internal memorandum from the Florida Department of Children and Families in the appendix that summarizes how the front line Medicaid personnel are supposed to implement the new changes.

Changes to transfer penalty rules.

At the heart of all the changes is a change to how and when a person is disqualified for benefits if they made any gifts prior to going into the nursing home. To understand the scope and effect of this new law a short review of how things used to be will help us understand how it is now. Prior to the new law if a person gave any assets away, whether or not they thought they might be going to a nursing home, they were disqualified for benefits. How long they would be disqualified depended on how much money was given away. For example, if $50,000 was given away then the person was disqualified for 10 months, if the amount was $100,000 they were disqualified for 20 months. The key here, however, is not necessarily how long the disqualification penalty period, but when the penalty period starts.

Now there is no such thing as an exempt minimum transfer. Under the old rules if the total amount of assets transferred in any given month was less than your state's penalty divisor, $5,000 for Florida, the transfers would not disqualify the applicant. Now, after implementation of the DRA, any transfer, regardless of size, disqualifies the applicant for a fraction of a month. Using a $5,000 divisor and breaking it down to days, an applicant is disqualified for one day for every $167 in gifts made. It is precisely this change coupled with the change in the penalty start date that creates the result of universal disqualification. Who has not given something away within the last five years?

Under the old law the period of disqualification started immediately after the giving of the gift. The result of this was that small gifts never disqualified an applicant for long, if at all. Even more substantial gifts, if made long enough before application, would not result in disqualification.

Now, however, under the new law signed by President Bush on February 8, 2006, each and every gift a person makes for the five years prior to their entry into the nursing home is added together as a "super transfer." The person will now be disqualified not from the date the transfer was made, but from the date he or she enters the nursing home, exhausts all remaining assets and applies for

Medicaid. The penalty for giving something away is imposed when the person needs benefits the most when they need care, are in the nursing home and have no money left to pay the bill. (Note that the five year look-back started in most states from February 8, 2006, meaning that it will take until 2011 for it to equal a full five year look-back period.)

An example may help. Mr. Smith over the last five years gave each of his three children a $500 gift for Christmas, made a weekly tithe to his church of $20, gave a one time gift of $1,000 to the Red Cross for hurricane relief, and $1,000 to the Republican party. When Mr. Smith goes into the nursing home he still has $25,000 in the bank. Under the new rules Mr. Smith will first have to spend the $25,000 on his nursing home care (about 4 months) until he reaches $2,000, then he can apply for Medicaid benefits. But, because of the transfers/gifts that he made, totaling $14,700, he will be disqualified for Medicaid for the next 4 months and 12 days. It is not clear where he will come up with the money to pay the nursing home for this period. The law is silent on this particular issue.

Mr. Smith's dilemma also may create the unintended result of placing our entire health care system in peril. The new law has also been referred to as the Nursing Home Bankruptcy Act of 2005 because of the effect it will have on nursing homes and their ability to get paid for the care they provide. In the example above, Mr. Smith, in most circumstances, cannot be discharged from the nursing home if he does not pay his bill. For those 4 months and 12 days the nursing home will be forced to care for the person without payment.

The result of this non-payment on the nursing home is clear. If they don't get paid for the care they are providing, they cannot stay in business. So what does the nursing home do? Do they stop taking patients that may go onto Medicaid? This is impossible, on average, seventy-five percent of a typical nursing home's clients are on Medicaid. Where does the person who is disqualified for benefits and who runs out of money go? In many cases the buck gets passed, and it is back to the hospital emergency room.

The hospital now has the patient but cannot discharge the person to the nursing home if the nursing home refuses to take the patient back. Other nursing homes are not interested in taking a patient with no way to pay for care, nor can the hospital discharge the patient to the street corner. Thus, the hospital fills up with non-dischargeable patients and cannot take new patients. If they cannot take new patients the hospital effectively closes and the cascade effect continues. The law of unintended consequences may ultimately act to close our hospitals by making it financially impossible for nursing homes to accept patients who may have made some form of transfer within the last five years. With no place for the hospital to discharge patients the hospitals will fill up and be unable to take new patients. Clearly the new law creates a lot of uncertainty and a possible rocky road ahead for patients, nursing homes and hospitals.

Increasing the look-back period.

A significant change in the rules contained within DRA 2005 is the increase in the look-back period for transfers from three years to five years. Now all transfers, whether to individuals or trusts, will be subject to a five year look-back period. Any transfer of assets within the look-back period must be disclosed at the time of application. The implementation of this rule is a little tricky. Since it went into effect in most states in February of 2006 it will take five years to come into complete effect. We will have a steadily increasing look-back period until we reach 2011 when there will finally be five years to look back for transfers. It is interesting to note that as of 2010 the state of Florida still only has a 36 month look-back period, having not fully implemented that part of the DRA, although this is likely to change.

Annuities are bad for planning.

The purchase of particular kinds of annuities known as immediate and their cousins balloon annuities were once a common asset protection strategy. They were used as a way to make assets non-countable for Medicaid eligibility, but under the DRA they are now being counted as assets. They can still be made to be a non-countable asset, but at an awfully high cost. In order to make the annuity into a non-counted asset, you must make the state the beneficiary of the annuity so that when the annuity owner dies the state receives the balance of the funds left in the annuity. Having to make the state the beneficiary of the annuity makes this strategy a rather unappealing method for asset protection.

The exact language of the DRA reads that the state "be named the remainder beneficiary in the first position for at least the total amount of medical assistance paid on behalf of the annuitant." This appears to mean that the state could demand the entire annuity even though the Medicaid beneficiary received only a month of Medicaid benefits.

There is also a question whether or not current Medicaid recipients have to change their existing annuities to make the state the beneficiary when their case comes up for annual recertification review. It is for these reasons that we now discourage the use of annuities in Medicaid planning situations in nearly every circumstance.

DRA and the home.

The sanctity of the home has also been attacked by the new law. The home's value was not counted under the old law. Under the new law there is now a cap on the maximum value of the applicant's home. If the home is valued at more than $500,000 the person is not eligible for Medicaid benefits. There is a provision that may allow the value cap to be raised to $750,000, on a state-by-state basis.

To further add to the confusion, the new law is being implemented at different times in different states. For example, the law was drafted in 2005, signed in 2006, but put into effect in Florida on November 1, 2007. This date is very important as it represents a division in how to assess any Medicaid case, using the old rules or the new depending on when the particular event, like a transfer, took place. In other states the effective date is February 8, 2006. Again, you will need to check your particular state's implementation date as this is critical in the eligibility analysis.

After DRA 2005 is Medicaid dead on arrival? No, despite the drastic changes in the law, Medicaid is still available to pay for long-term care. It has been made much more difficult to qualify and there are many more ways to be disqualified, but with proper planning and guidance Medicaid continues to be a viable method to pay the nursing home. In many ways the new changes have made the assistance of the elder law attorney even more imperative.

It is clear that things will now be very different in the world of Medicaid and nursing home care. The new law has completely changed the landscape of Medicaid benefits, but many solutions still exist to solve these seemingly unsolvable problems, protect the person's assets and qualify for Medicaid. As with any Medicaid law there are sure to be more changes as the law is further interpreted. Keep updated by visiting www.virtuallawoffice.com.

Key Point. What you need to know about The Deficit Reduction Act of 2005:

- Changes the look-back period to five years.
- Changes the penalty start date to date of application.
- Adds fractional disqualification. (Partial months.)
- Curtails the use of annuities.
- Implementation date is critical, check your state.
- Limits the value of the home to $500,000.

CHAPTER **5**
TRANSFERRING ASSETS

●●

In this chapter:

Why you can't give assets away.
Do you go to jail for transferring assets?
How to determine periods of disqualification.
What is a look-back period?

●●

Transferring assets violates the first commandment of Medicaid law, that "Thou shalt not give your assets away to qualify for Medicaid benefits." If the applicant has too many assets and wants to qualify for Medicaid, the tendency for most people is to give the excess assets away, usually to a family member. This solution sounds too easy, and as with most things, if it sounds too easy, you can't do it.

The government will not allow you to simply give assets away in order to become qualified for benefits. There are very strict rules prohibiting gifts of assets to become eligible for Medicaid. Any uncompensated transfer or even an under-compensated transfer will disqualify the applicant from receiving Medicaid benefits.

Assets may be moved and preserved if done in a way the rules allow. It cannot be a gift or a transfer, but nonetheless the assets can be moved, and if moved properly the assets become protected. This is the essence of Medicaid planning, the moving of assets to preserve and protect them without offending Medicaid's rules. Permissible asset movements are discussed more fully in the "Strategies" section to follow.

It is not a crime to transfer assets to become eligible for Medicaid benefits although Congress has tried in the past to put you in jail for giving assets away. In January 1997, for example, legislation attempted to make it a crime to transfer assets to become eligible for benefits. This law came to be known as the Granny Goes to Jail Law. The public outrage forced Congress to amend the law. Congress's next attempt at Medicaid criminalization made it a crime for someone, even your attorney, to tell a client how to legally transfer assets in order to qualify for benefits. It was as if they were saying that while it was legal to transfer assets it would be illegal to tell anyone about it. The absurdity of such a law has been recognized by the courts and has been overturned for restricting constitutionally guaranteed free speech. Currently, the law is prohibited from further enforcement.

The most recent changes to Medicaid law under the Deficit Reduction Act of 2005, while not making it a crime to give assets away, make the transfer of assets fatal to Medicaid qualification.

Transfer Ineligibility

Generally, giving assets away disqualifies the person applying for benefits. If someone does give assets away, how long does the person have to wait before he or she can become eligible for Medicaid? This is a fundamental question for many people. The law concerning transfers of assets took a dramatic turn against the interest of seniors. In February 2006, President Bush overhauled Medicaid law signing legislation that completely changed how Medicaid applicants would be penalized for giving assets away.

The core change is that after the implementation of the new law, the Medicaid applicant is penalized from the date that he or she applies for Medicaid benefits after he or she enters the nursing home AND, but for the transfer penalty, would otherwise be eligible for Medicaid benefits. Prior to the new law the penalty period simply began running on the date the gift of was made. The implementation date is extremely important when assessing eligibility for Medicaid as it dramatically changes how to treat a transfer of assets.

The amount of time the person has to wait for benefits to begin paying for care (the penalty period) is calculated by dividing the amount of assets transferred by the average cost of care in a nursing home as defined by each state. This average cost of care figure, also known as the penalty divisor, does not usually reflect the actual current average cost of care, but is simply a part of the state's formula used to determine the ineligibility period.

Key Point. To determine the length of time an improper transfer disqualifies someone from Medicaid benefits , take the amount of money transferred and divide by your state's transfer penalty divisor. (Florida's is $5,000.) The resulting answer is the number of months the person is ineligible for Medicaid. The ineligibility starts from the date of application for Medicaid benefits, after entry into the nursing home, after the applicant has reached the $2,000 asset level, has an income trust in place if needed and otherwise would meet all the other requirements to be eligible for Medicaid.

In Florida, the penalty divisor is set at $5,000 per month. Under the new law, if you transferred $50,000 to your son within the look-back period of 60 months, you would be ineligible for benefits for a period of ten months from the date of application for Medicaid. (50,000 ÷ 5,000 = 10 months.)

Prior to the new law if a person gave any assets away they were disqualified for benefits starting at the date of the transfer. The transfer penalty clock started to tick when the money was given away. If the amount of the gift was not sufficient to result in at least one month of disqualification the penalty period was rounded down to zero months of disqualification. As a result, small gifts never disqualified an applicant.

Now, under the new law signed by President Bush on February 8, 2006, each and every gift a person makes, no matter how small during the five years prior to the person's entry into the nursing home, is added together to create a "super transfer." This super transfer is then divided by the penalty divisor to calculate the amount of disqualification time. The person is disqualified not from the date the transfer was made, but from the date he or she applies for Medicaid after entering the nursing home. In other words, the penalty for giving something away is imposed when the person needs the benefits the most, when they enter the nursing home.

The question of when the transfer occurred is critical to determining the disqualification period. Did the transfer happen before or after the implementation date of the new law. The implementation date changes from state to state so make sure you determine when your particular state began implementation of the new rules. In Florida for example, the effective date for the implementation of the new rules was November 1, 2007. For those transfers done before that date you use the old rules where the penalty started the date the gift was made. If the transfer happened after the implementation date, use the new method and calculate the period from the date of entry into the nursing home.

A few examples may help: Ms. Spendalot, a Florida, resident, gave her son $20,000 on June 1, 2007. She knew she was likely to go to a nursing home at some point. Six months later, on January 1, 2008, she entered the nursing home and applied for Medicaid. Did the earlier transfer of $20,000 hurt her? Assuming that the effective date for implementation of the new rules is November 1, 2007 (Florida's date), she is okay and eligible for benefits. The key here is that Ms. Spendalot made the transfer before the effective date of the new rules and was therefore subject to the old method of penalty calculation. Under the old rules her penalty started on June 2007 and disqualified her for the next four months ($20,000/5000 = 4 months). Six months have passed since the transfer, therefore she is okay and is no longer disqualified for Medicaid.

If you change the dates in this example to after the effective date of the new rules, so that the date of transfer was June 1, 2008 and the entry into the nursing home was six months later on January 1, 2009, the picture changes dramatically. Instead of being eligible for benefits four months after the date of the transfer, Ms. Spendalot's penalty period does not start until she enters the nursing home, has less than $2,000 in assets, her income is below the income cap, and she has applied and been denied eligibility for Medicaid benefits. The penalty therefore starts not on June 1, 2008, but instead on January 1, 2009 making her disqualified until May of 2009! Instead of being disqualified for four months from the date of transfer, she effectively must wait for 10 months after she gave her assets away.

The amount of time she must wait depends on the amount of her transfers and the date she enters the nursing home. Applicants under the new law are not only disqualified for big transfers, small transfers also add up to wreak havoc on eligibility.

To see how small transfers, and the existence of assets at the time of application act to disqualify applicants let's fast-forward five years into the future and take a look at Mr. Jones' case. Mr. Jones, over the previous five years, starting January 1, 2008, gave each of his four children a $500 gift for Christmas, he made a weekly tithe to his church of $20, gave a one-time gift of $1,000 to the Red Cross for hurricane relief, and $1,000 to his favorite political candidate. When Mr. Jones goes into the nursing home in January 2013 he still has $25,000 in the bank. Under the new rules Mr. Jones will first have to spend the $25,000 on his nursing home care (about 4 months) until he reaches $2,000 in assets. Only after spending down this money can he become eligible for Medicaid benefits. But, because of the small transfers and gifts that he made over the past five years, (totaling $17,200) he will be disqualified for Medicaid as if he made a lump sum transfer and must pay privately for the next 3 months and 12 days ($17,200/5000 = 3.44 months).

Where will Mr. Smith come up with the money to pay the nursing home during his period of disqualification? The disqualification period not only penalizes the applicant, but it also penalizes the nursing home. Picture Mr. Smith in the nursing home, having spent all his funds on his care, waiting out his disqualification period with the nursing home being left to continue to provide care without getting paid. Repeat this situation for nearly every potential Medicaid applicant and you get a disaster. The average nursing home has at any given time about 75 percent of its residents being paid for by Medicaid. If Medicaid is not an option for payment, the person has no more money, the family is tapped out struggling under their own financial demands, who pays for the care? The nursing home cannot continue to function if it is not being paid for the care it provides.

There are some transfers that will not disqualify the applicant. As of the printing of this book inter-spousal transfers, movement of assets between spouses, are not considered transfers. No penalties are assessed for transferring assets between husband and wife. Additionally, gifts to a disabled child will not disqualify the applicant, but may have a negative affect on the child's own eligibility requiring additional planning. And finally, gifts to a specific type of trust called a pooled trust will not disqualify the applicant.

Look-Back Periods

The transfer of asset penalty disqualifies the applicant only if he or she transfers assets within a certain period of time before applying for benefits. This period of time is called a look-back period. Previously there were two look-back periods; one that went back 36 months, the other 60 months. Under the new law there is only one look-back period. Any transfer or gift made within a 60 month period prior to application must be disclosed during the application process. The new look-back period starts at the implementation date but will take five years to be fully implemented.

A good way to visualize the concept of a look-back period is to think of a time line.

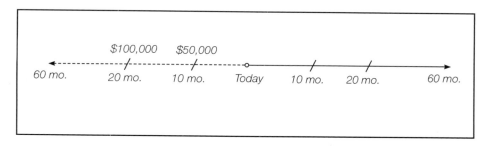

Look-back period time line.

Any transfer that falls within the past 60 months must be disclosed at the time of the application for benefits. In the illustration above, if a $50,000 transfer was made 10 months ago, it must be disclosed at the time of the Medicaid application. Similarly, a transfer of $100,000 made 20 months ago must be disclosed. Whether or not the applicant is disqualified depends on when the transfer was made. Remember the transfer does not necessarily have to be one big transfer. It can be an aggregate of all the transfers made by the applicant in the prior five years before the application.

Transferring or giving assets away is one of the most basic techniques used to qualify for Medicaid. Transfers under the new law, however, almost guarantees denial. In order to successfully

obtain benefits by an out-right transfer of assets, you must
accurately predict the future. You must know when you will need to
go into the nursing home. Such a prediction is usually impossible.
It is for this reason that we will rarely recommend an outright
transfer of assets when assisting clients qualify for Medicaid.
Instead, we will utilize one or a combination of other strategies
to obtain eligibility. These strategies reposition the client's assets
without the movement of assets being defined as a disqualifying
transfer.

CHAPTER 6
INCOME AND ELIGIBILITY

●●●

In this chapter:

The importance of a good durable power of attorney.
Making the income cap disappear.
How income flows through an income trust.
The Spousal Diversion.

●●●

The goal of every good Medicaid planning strategy is to preserve the most assets while obtaining eligibility as soon as possible. In order to accomplish this you need to first start with an accurate assessment of the applicant's assets and income. Many states only look at the assets of the applicant to determine eligibility, while others, like Florida, require the applicant's income AND assets be below the cap amounts. Review your state's particular requirements in the appendix.

The importance of a good durable power of attorney.

When long-term care becomes an issue it is often because the person can no longer provide for their own care. The same problems that put a person into a nursing home are often the same problems that remove his or her capacity to act on his or her own behalf. There must be a plan in place before the loss of capacity occurs that appoints a "second in command." The appointment is most often accomplished with a durable power of attorney.

Perhaps the most important component of Medicaid planning is a good durable power of attorney. A durable power of attorney is a document that grants authority to a designated person to act on behalf of another. The power of attorney's function is to avoid the problems created when someone loses capacity. Without a power of attorney no one is available to act on behalf of the incapacitated person. Once the person becomes incapacitated or incompetent it is too late to have them sign a durable power of attorney. In cases where the opportunity to get a power of attorney has passed, a court appointed guardian can act on behalf of the incapacitated individual. Setting up a guardianship is a time-consuming and expensive process. Even though a guardianship can be instituted, Medicaid planning done under the auspices of a guardianship is more difficult and costly.

Not just any power of attorney will do. The tendency is to think that all powers of attorney are the same. They simply are not. In the context of Medicaid planning, the specific terms and limitations of the particular power of attorney document can have far reaching effects. Many powers of attorney that we see either expressly, or by reference and incorporation of statutes, prohibit trust creation, or prohibit or limit the ability to make gifts, sell homes, or access IRAs to name a few deficiencies. A poorly drafted power of attorney may not allow you to do the things necessary to become eligible for Medicaid benefits. Specificity is the key in power of attorney drafting. The more specific the better. The age of the document is also a factor. Older documents are more likely to be rejected than newer ones. The document needs to clearly describe what the attorney-in-fact can do. (The attorney-in-fact is the person who steps into the shoes of the incapacitated person.) Broad language that states the attorney-in-fact can do anything that the person could have done if competent is not good enough.

In the majority of my cases I find that the power of attorney document is usually defective in some critical way that requires the document to be updated. Too often we see limiting language or the absence of language regarding the powers granted to the attorney-in-fact. Make sure your documents are current, and are competently drafted. Review your documents with an experienced elder law attorney before the loss of capacity ties your hands. Remember, after capacity is gone, so is the opportunity to get or fix a power of attorney.

Reality Check. A recent client's father with advanced Alzheimer's disease was in a nursing home. The father had too much income to qualify for benefits. He had a durable power of attorney but the document did not have language allowing for the creation of trusts. The son therefore had no authority to create an income trust.

Without the correct language the son's ability to help his father was thwarted. The only alternative was to begin a guardianship, a costly and time-consuming court proceeding.

Review your DPOA. Does it specifically state that the person can create an income trust?

Making the income cap disappear - Income Trusts

If the applicant is in an income cap state like Florida and is over the income cap, he or she is not eligible for Medicaid benefits. To fix this problem an income trust needs to be created and properly funded. An income trust does not protect assets, it only reduces the income of the applicant below the cap amount. It does, however, allow you to satisfy the income requirement so you can move on to preserving assets.

If the applicant is over the income cap and wants to qualify for Medicaid he or she must have an income trust drafted, executed and properly funded in the month that he or she wants benefits to begin.

The concept of an income trust is relatively simple. A trust is created by the attorney and signed by the applicant, the applicant's spouse or the applicant's power of attorney. Next, a checking account is opened in the trust's name at a local bank. Then every month thereafter, the applicant's income is moved from the applicant's individual bank account to the trust's checking account. The minimum amount moved must be enough to bring the applicant's income below the income cap.

The chart below illustrates the movement of income from the applicant to the nursing home, including the use of the income trust to take the excess income and the distribution of some of the income to a community spouse as a spousal diversion.

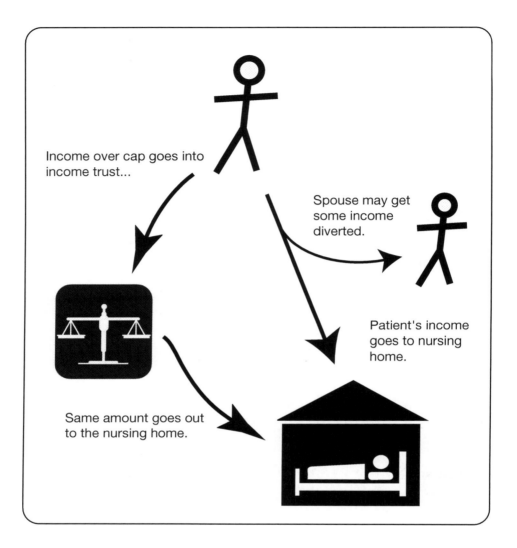

Income over cap goes into income trust...

Spouse may get some income diverted.

Patient's income goes to nursing home.

Same amount goes out to the nursing home.

Income over the income cap flows from the applicant to the nursing home through an income trust.

In Florida, the 2010 income cap is $2,022 per month. So, for example, if the applicant has $2,023 in monthly income, the applicant is over the cap by $1 and will need to put at least $1 into the trust each month in order to get below the income limit. After the income trust receives the applicant's income, it turns around and pays the income to the nursing home as part of the overall patient's responsibility. Remember the applicant must pay all of his or her income to the nursing home each month. The income trust acts only as a pass through. Nothing stays in the income trust.

Jargon Cutter. The term "patient responsibility" refers to the amount the nursing home resident is required to pay to the nursing home every month. It is generally equal to the applicant's gross monthly income minus a $35 personal needs allowance (PNA) and in the cases where there is a community spouse, a deduction for the spouse.

The Spousal Diversion

In the income trust diagram note the share that is diverted over to the spouse. This is known as a spousal diversion or a minimum monthly maintenance income allowance (MMMIA). This diverted amount was designed to supplement the spouse who has a low income. In 2010, a Florida spouse's income will usually need to be below $1,822 per month in order to receive any diversion. The spouse's minimum income limit for diversion changes from state-to-state so be sure to localize this information to your particular jurisdiction.

Use the following worksheet to get a general idea of how much spousal diversion may be allotted in your particular case and what the spouse is likely to have as a total monthly income. Add the income the spouse receives from all sources for line "a". Add all shelter costs, including your state's utility allowance, to get line "b". (Florida's 2010 amount is $198.) 30% of the MMMIA, line "e" has been calculated for you but will change depending on what your particular state's MMMIA is. Next, subtract line "b" from line "c" to the get the excess shelter costs. This amount will be added to the MMMIA to assist with the cost of providing a home for the community spouse. Add line "d" and line "e" to determine the spousal diversion amount. And finally add line "f" and "a" to determine the spouse's total projected monthly income. If you want to get really fancy, subtract the spousal diversion amount from the applicant's income to determine the patient's responsibility.

INCOME		
Social Security		
Pension + Other Income		
Interest Income (estimated)		
TOTAL GROSS INCOME FOR COMMUNITY SPOUSE		a
SHELTER COSTS		
Rent or Mortgage		
Taxes		
Insurance		
Maintenance		
Utility Allowance	$198.00	
SUBTOTAL OF SHELTER COSTS		b
30% MMMIA	($525.00)	c
EXCESS SHELTER COSTS		d
	(d = b-c)	
MMMIA	$1,822.00	e
SPOUSAL DIVERSION		f
	(f = d+e)	
COMMUNITY SPOUSE INCOME ALLOWANCE		g
	(g = f-a)	

Spousal Diversion Calculation Worksheet (2010)

CHAPTER 7
ASSET PRESERVATION STRATEGIES

● ●

In this chapter:

Transfers, the good, the bad and the ugly.

Asset conversion, countable to non-countable.

Annuities, life insurance and loans.

Personal Care Contracts.

Spousal Refusal.

Pooled Trusts.

Hardship.

● ●

When seeking qualification for Medicaid benefits to pay for the nursing home one of the first questions I ask is what are the total countable assets of the applicant and applicant's spouse? If the amount of the applicant's assets is above the eligibility threshold enough assets must be repositioned to reduce the total countable assets below the asset cap amount. In most cases all the applicant's excess assets can be repositioned so as to qualify for Medicaid benefits. This is generally regardless of the amount or type of assets. It is just a matter of how and when to do it.

When meeting with clients it is our standard procedure to analyze the client's entire situation to determine the proper course of action. We take into account the character of the assets, the amount, the particulars of the family situation and the individual goals of each client.

The character of the asset is important. Whether it is jointly owned, tax qualified, or highly appreciated will all affect the particular choice of strategy. The composition of the family including the prospective needs of the spouse or children will influence the planning process as well. And finally, the goals of the client concerning the preservation of assets ultimately dictate the final plan of action.

Before you start Medicaid planning, it is a good idea to know the total amount of your assets. Below is a simple worksheet to help you get an idea where you are starting from and the amount of assets to be protected.

ASSET TYPE	$ AMOUNT
Cash (checking, savings, cd's)	
Stocks/Bonds	
Annuities	
Real Property (other than home)	
Cars	
IRAs and 401k	
TOTAL ASSETS	
Subtract asset cap amount	See your states particular amount.
AMOUNT TO BE PROTECTED	

Asset Protection Worksheet.

Once you know what and how much is at risk, you can take action to protect it. Each client presents a different set of facts and requires a unique set of techniques to preserve his or her assets. There is definitely no "cookie cutter" solution to solving the over asset problem.

The Medicaid laws and the nuance of their application in individual cases require the guidance of an elder law attorney, period, no getting around it. Unfortunately, this book cannot completely convey my 20 years of experience in its few pages. You may on occasion get lucky trying to preserve assets without assistance, but rarely will the optimal set of solutions be used.

In order to ensure eligibility, a custom strategy for each particular client must be correctly implemented with the help of an experienced elder law attorney. I have been faulted for making this point in the past as some sort of self serving statement. While qualification for Medicaid benefits can be a simple matter in some cases, most are much more complex. Despite the wish that there be some easy method that I could impart to you within these pages to qualify for benefits, the fact of the matter is your circumstances are unique to you and require a unique solution to optimally obtain Medicaid benefits.

I must stress that no book on the general subject of nursing home financing and asset preservation can provide a step-by-step recipe for Medicaid qualification. Those that purport to tell you the secrets to Medicaid qualification are dangerous and can instead produce the exact opposite result of Medicaid *dis*qualification. The reason for this is the different interpretation and implementation of the Medicaid rules across the 50 states.

Each state and sometimes even each county within a state can have widely differing interpretations of the Medicaid rules. Local knowledge is not just helpful, but absolutely critical in obtaining a positive outcome.

There are few things in life as dangerous as a little information. Unfortunately, the nature of any book is that it can only convey so much information. It is impossible to put every possible situation and or combination of situations in the limited space represented by this guide. It is my hope that the following discussion of some asset preservation strategies will help you see the possibilities that exist to help protect a life-time of savings.

> Key Point. Medicaid eligibility strategies change drastically from state to state. Since each state has some decision in how Medicaid is implemented in that state, wide variations in allowable asset preservation strategies are created.

Each and every strategy discussed below may or may not be allowed in your particular state. I have said it elsewhere, but I will repeat: You must get competent advice from an elder law attorney in your particular state before embarking on any of the following strategies.

Asset Transfers

The transfer of assets is generally frowned upon by Medicaid. There are, however, multiple strategies that exist to move assets in order to protect them. One very basic strategy, called a transfer and wait strategy, is simplicity in action. First an assessment is made to determine the amount to be moved to put the future Medicaid applicant within the eligibility standards, then that amount is transferred to a third party, typically a child or other family member. This transfer though, by its very nature, can disqualify the person for benefits for a significant period of time. This is not one of my favorite strategies because it requires the client to be able to predict the future date when the person will need nursing home care. But, in the right circumstances, with enough advance warning, the transfer and wait strategy can be effective.

In most jurisdictions a large transfer of assets can result in a 60 month disqualification. With enough lead time though, you can transfer an unlimited amount of assets and wait the full 60 month look-back period before applying. In some jurisdictions there is still only a 36 month look-back period. As of the printing of this book, Florida was using a 36 month look-back period.

The new federal Medicaid laws have made it very dangerous to give anything away, even birthday presents and church tithes, without negatively affecting Medicaid eligibility. We are currently advising our clients interested in Medicaid qualification to stop making any form of transfer or gift without specific guidance from our office. Making gifts of any kind can have disastrous effects on eligibility, caution and guidance are highly recommended.

Incremental, small, asset transfer strategies, where you move assets on a monthly basis instead of a lump sum, until recently were a favored method of asset preservation for clients who were pre-planning for a future nursing home placement. A good example would be where one spouse has Alzheimer's disease but is still able to be at home for the foreseeable future. In this case we would begin a drain of the assets by transferring a specific amount of assets each month just under the amount that would disqualify the client. This technique, however, no longer works after the recent law changes under DRA 2005. Each small monthly movement of assets now is added together to form a super transfer with the penalty being assessed at the time of Medicaid application based upon the total amount transferred. These small disqualifying transfers can even include Christmas gifts and charitable donations.

Watch out! Even small micro transfers add up to large periods of disqualification under the DRA. There is no minimum amount that can be transferred without penalty. Church tithes, birthday presents, charitable contributions and political contributions of any size disqualify the applicant.

As discussed elsewhere in this book the issue of penalty calculations for the transfer of assets is a critical concept to understand. Some points to reiterate are that: There is no automatic penalty of 36 or 60 months for the transfer of assets. The penalty is a calculated penalty based upon the amount that was improperly transferred. Under Florida law there is generally one month of disqualification for every $5,000 transferred. This $5,000 figure is referred to as the penalty divisor and can be different from state to state.

Transfer Penalty Start Date

Prior to the date that the Deficit Reduction Act was implemented in your state, November 1, 2007 in Florida, disqualification penalty periods began to elapse when the transfer was made. Under recent changes to the Medicaid laws, disqualification penalty periods now only start after three things happen: The applicant is in the nursing home, he or she is within the financial eligibility requirements for Medicaid, and the applicant has applied and been denied Medicaid benefits. When evaluating your case the date the transfer was made is very important in calculating the penalty period. This change in the penalty start date produces dramatically different results depending on when the transfer was made.

Even though transfers are usually counterproductive to becoming eligible for benefits, given enough notice and lead time, the simple strategy of transferring sufficient assets and waiting out the penalty period becomes a possible option. Depending on your state, that maximum waiting period will either be five years or three. The state of Florida, at the present time, has a three year waiting period, while most states, after the implementation of the Deficit Reduction Act, now have a five year period.

Small Transfers and Fractional Disqualification

Under the law of Medicaid prior to the introduction and implementation of the Deficit Reduction Act small monthly transfers or gifts of assets did not disqualify the Medicaid applicant. Prior to the implementation of the Deficit Reduction Act, you could make a transfer of assets up to the maximum amount of the monthly penalty divisor ($5,000 in Florida) and not trigger any disqualification. If less than $5,000 was given away a fraction of a month of disqualification would be created. Fractions of a month were not counted and resulted in no penalty or disqualification. Under the new law however, even small transfers create disqualification penalties. There no longer exists any safe amount of uncompensated transfer that will not otherwise disqualify the applicant. A $5,000 transfer causes one month of ineligibility, a $2,500 transfer causes 15 days of ineligibility and a $167 transfer creates one day of ineligibility. It is important to note that small transfers can accumulate to disqualify the applicant from benefits for multiple months.

Transfer Tax Issues

There are many factors to consider when making transfers, not the least of which is tax law. Tax law and Medicaid law crash into each other on this issue. Gift tax law limits the amount that can be given away to $13,000 per person per year FOR TAX PURPOSES. If you go over this amount a gift tax return (form 709) must be filed. Many people take this tax law and try to apply it to Medicaid only to find out that while you can make that $13,000 or smaller transfer without any tax consequences, the same transfer violates Medicaid's rules and disqualifies the applicant from Medicaid benefits.

There are other tax issues including capital gains and income tax issues to consider when giving assets away. The recipient of the gift receives the cost basis of the item gifted. For example, if the recipient gets appreciated stock, the capital gains will be calculated at time of sale using the original cost of the stock, usually resulting in higher capital gains than if the stock would have been received as a distribution from the applicant's estate. The difference in tax treatment can be substantial in this case. Income tax also comes into consideration. You cannot gift tax deferred assets without paying income tax. Examples of tax deferred assets would be a 401K, IRAs, and tax deferred annuities. Should you give a tax deferred asset away the income tax becomes due immediately.

What exactly constitutes a transfer can be a tough question. Disqualifying transfers can happen even when it does not look like a transfer, for instance, simply adding someone's name to a deed creates a transfer, but, adding someone to your checking account does not, but, should that person then take money out of the joint account, then that is a transfer. As you can see transfers can get tricky. Making a gift or uncompensated transfer of assets is the easiest way to disqualify the applicant.

Curing Bad Transfers

The good news is that if you do make a gift or transfer that disqualifies you for benefits you can fix that problem by curing the gift. You cure the gift by making a re-transfer of the gift back to the applicant. The amount re-transferred goes back to the applicant effectively resetting the penalty clock. This gets rid of the penalty, but puts you back into a position of having too many assets. Once the money is given back then you can proceed forward with moving it through a permissible, non-disqualifying strategy.

Key Point. If you transfer assets, whether for the purpose to become eligible for Medicaid or not, but need benefits before the penalty period has elapsed, you can undo the transfer penalty by giving the assets back and moving them through another technique.

Permissible Transfers

Some transfers are okay. Transfers back and forth between spouses are non-disqualifying regardless of the amount or when they are made. In many cases the transfer or realignment of assets into the community spouse's name is actually required. In these cases the transfer can be made after eligibility is determined, usually within 90 days of the applicant's approval. While transfers to a community spouse are not a disqualifying event, should the community spouse end up with more than he or she is allowed to have, the applicant will still be ineligible for benefits. In spousal situations there is no look-back period to be concerned with. Transfers can be made at any time. These transfers are important to reduce the amount of assets in the applicant spouse's name below the asset limit, typically $2,000. There is an added benefit in that the income produced from the asset follows the transfer thereby reducing the amount of income attributable to the applicant spouse. Such a reduction may be necessary to reduce the applicant's income below the required limits in an income cap state such as Florida.

A Medicaid applicant can also make penalty free transfers to a blind or disabled child. Disability is defined as the inability to work, which condition is likely to last at least a year. A determination by Social Security, while not necessary, will definitively establish that the person is disabled. Caution is advised though. Many times the proposed recipient is receiving public benefits themselves, or may need to access public benefits in the future. A transfer to that child could jeopardize his or her own present or potential eligibility.

Reality Check. Within this last year I had a client in a nursing home with a difficult situation. She had a significant amount of assets and she was very old. She had her only daughter of 61 years of age, with Down's syndrome, residing with her in the same nursing home. Transferring the assets to the disabled daughter would make the mother eligible for benefits but would destroy the daughter's eligibility for her own Medicaid benefits.

In this case a special needs trust was created by the mother for the benefit of the disabled daughter. Nearly all the mother's assets were then transferred to the special needs trust. And viola! The mother qualified for benefits immediately with the daughter also retaining her eligibility. A transfer to a special needs trust for the benefit of the disabled child does not count as a transfer.

While a disabled child can present a planning opportunity, care must be taken to avoid disqualifying the child from his or her own benefits.

Half-A-Loaf Transfer

One transfer strategy that has been available since the change in Medicaid rules in 1988 has been the half-a-loaf strategy. The half-a-loaf name is a reference to splitting the assets in half with one half protected and the other half "consumed" while waiting for the penalty period to expire. In order to implement this strategy in the new post DRA Medicaid world, first all the assets are transferred, then go through the steps necessary to trigger the penalty period (be in the nursing home, all other requirements met, apply and get denied) and finally, give back half of the assets to reduce the penalty period by half. During the penalty period you use the returned funds to pay the long-term care expenses. A variation of the half-a-loaf uses a pooled trust strategy to give half the assets away with the other half going to a pooled trust. The first transfer creates a penalty while the transfer to the pooled trust does not. The pooled trust then makes the long term care payments during the period of disqualification.

Transfer of Exempt Assets

Most exempt assets can be transferred without a penalty. A transfer of a vehicle, for example, would not be a disqualifying transfer. The rules state, however, that the exempt homestead and real property made exempt because it was listed for sale CANNOT be transferred under this exception.

Transferring the Home

When it comes to transferring the homestead, special rules apply. The following are some instances where the transfer of the home will not disqualify the applicant from benefits:

- Transfer to a blind, disabled or dependent child under 21
- Transfer to a sibling with an equity interest in the home who resided in the home for one year or more
- Transfer to a child who has resided in the home for the past 2 years and who provided care that delayed long-term care placement

As you can see transferring assets can often result in disqualification, but that in some cases there is some room to maneuver.

Some other common transfer mistakes to avoid:

- Make sure to triple check the date when the transfer was made. Finding yourself still within the look-back period can create a penalty longer than the 36 or 60 month look-back period.
- Adding a name to a piece of real property will usually be considered a transfer.
- Consider that a transferred asset may not be protected if the person who you transfer the asset to uses or abuses that asset. It could be gone.

Other examples of transfer strategies discussed below include paying the assets to a family member, moving it to a specialized pooled trust or loaning the asset out. Within each of these strategies there are multiple variations that can be used to customize the solution to the unique needs of the applicant.

Conversion Strategies and Exempt Assets

The general planning concept behind many a Medicaid asset protection strategy revolves around the concept of exempt assets versus countable assets. The general idea is to convert or change the character of a countable asset into an exempt, non-countable asset.

Joint Ownership

Owning certain types of property jointly with another can move that property out of the countable column. Two joint property examples include jointly held real property and jointly titled stock. Both assets if owned jointly with another person require two signatures to liquidate or sell the particular property. The refusal of one of the owners to sell the asset renders that asset unavailable to the applicant and makes it non-countable. The downside to this strategy is that the joint ownership must be created far enough back in time prior to application for benefits so that the creation of joint ownership falls outside the look-back period for transfers.

In contrast, a joint bank account where either party has access to the funds without the necessity of consent by the joint holder does not make the asset unavailable to the applicant and therefore will still be counted as the applicant's asset. As an additional caution, do not allow the joint holder of the bank account to make any transfers out of the account. Doing so will be the same as if the applicant had made the transfer thereby creating a transfer disqualification penalty.

The Home

Perhaps the largest exempt asset is the primary residence of the applicant. The primary residence or home of the applicant is not counted up to a maximum value of $500,000. This limit was a recent addition to Medicaid law introduced as part of the Deficit Reduction Act of 2005. Houses, town homes, apartments, condos, co-ops, mobile homes, even a motor home or houseboat can all qualify as a primary residence. The dual exempt status of a motor home as a vehicle and a home presents an interesting opportunity to avoid the $500,000 limitation on the value of a home. It may be possible to characterize that $750,000 Prevost motor home as your exempt car. So if your home is over the new cap, consider putting wheels on it!

> Key Point. The valuation of a home is subject to many factors and market conditions. The applicant must present proof of the home's value. Note, that the value of the home is reduced by any indebtedness on the property.

Assets can be protected by changing their character, essentially converting them from countable assets to non-countable. One example of asset conversion would include making improvements to the applicant's home. Any improvement paid for by countable cash assets is transformed into the home, a non-countable asset. The purchase of a new more expensive home shifts assets from being counted to being exempt. The purchase of a car would likewise change a countable asset into an exempt asset. The purchase of a burial or funeral contract is another example of permissible asset conversion. Asset conversion strategies have their use, and in the right situation can be very effective in preserving assets. These strategies can also be combined with other strategies to provide custom solutions to the asset preservation problem.

As with every strategy care must be taken in the implementation of the plan. Pitfalls to avoid include valuation of the home and making sure that you can establish the home as the primary residence of the applicant. The requirements of what makes the home a primary residence are vague and subject to interpretation. Generally, if you can show that the applicant resided in the home and could clearly demonstrate a continued intent to reside there by presenting facts such as a change of address on all mail, claiming any special tax exemptions related to a primary residence, homestead exemption in Florida for example, that the home was the address on the applicant's voter registration along with any other facts that tend to show the applicant has made the home his or her primary residence. Some facts that may lead to questioning whether the home is the primary residence include but are not limited to:

- That the property was purchased shortly before or after admission to the nursing home
- That there is reason to believe that the applicant did not live in the home because of an extended stay in an ALF or that he or she lived with children for an extended time prior to admission to the nursing home
- That the applicant owns multiple properties that could qualify as a home

Basically, you should use common sense when evaluating if a property is the principal place of residence. Property does not automatically become a home just because a nursing home resident is discharged for a "home" visit. You will need to have evidence that clearly indicates that the home served as the applicant's principle place of residence prior to admission to the nursing home. The applicant's home will continue to be excluded as an asset even during an extended absence if the applicant has an intent to return to the home.

Personal Property

Pots and pans are not things that Medicaid is interested in. Personal property such as household goods are not counted and are another example of an exempt asset. Jewelry, wedding rings, furniture, all the stuff in your life, is effectively not counted as an asset. The technical limitation contained within the rules is that the applicant is allowed $2,000 in personal household goods. There is a presumption however, that the applicant's personal property is worth only $1,000 unless you state otherwise. If the applicant is married then issue of valuation of personal property is reduced even further. In a married situation, all the personal property of the non-applying spouse is not counted. Due to the impossibility of establishing value and ownership of personal property, Medicaid effectively does not count its value when determining eligibility.

Burial Plans

A unique piece of personal property that is dealt with specifically within the Medicaid rules is the burial/funeral arrangement and plot. Contracts for burial and funerals are often thought to be non-countable assets. However, they are only excluded if they are made irrevocable. The amount paid for that contract will be a countable asset for purposes of determining eligibility for benefits until the contract is made irrevocable. I often refer to this as a great example of "gotcha law". In other words, you think you are okay, but at the time of application you are told that you are disqualified because you are over the asset level. In order for the burial contract not to be counted as an asset the contract must be irrevocable. In essence, if it is irrevocable, you cannot get a refund, so the money is not available to the Medicaid applicant. That one little word, irrevocable, makes all the difference. If the burial contract is not irrevocable, it can be made irrevocable by signing an assignment of pre-need funeral contract form that you can obtain from the funeral home.

Key Point. In order for the purchase price of a pre-paid burial contract not to be counted as an asset it must either be a non-refundable contract or be made irrevocable through the execution of an irrevocable assignment of pre-need funeral contract.

Additionally, up to $2,500 in a bank account can be excluded if it is designated for burial. Simply putting "for burial" on the account card at the bank will suffice. Make sure that you also make the account a joint account or a pay on death (POD) account so that the money can be easily accessed after the applicant's death. Note, that this account can grow above the $2,500 amount after the applicant has been approved for Medicaid benefits. The actual account can be any kind of account, CD, checking, or savings. Life insurance can also be designated for burial.

Vehicles

A Medicaid applicant can own one vehicle, either a car, truck, van, motor home, or motorcycle without that vehicle being counted as an asset. This vehicle will be excluded from being counted as part of the applicant's assets when determining if the applicant is within the magic target of eligibility. The purchase of a vehicle is a classic example of converting a countable asset into an exempt asset but it is not such a great asset preservation strategy since a vehicle is typically not a very good investment and usually depreciates in value pretty quickly. Still, in many cases when we need to position a small amount of money or when the need for a new vehicle is present, using a vehicle purchase is a quick and easy way to reach the eligibility level.

An applicant is not limited to only one vehicle, any vehicle over seven years old is also excluded as an asset. I often get asked if the owner/applicant has to be able to drive the car, my reply is to reference the movie Driving Miss Daisy. The applicant is not required to even have a valid driver's license. As a practical matter when you are sitting at the dealership you will need insurance on the vehicle before you can drive it home. Vehicles can be owned by one party and registered in another's name, As an alternative, you can title the car in joint names.

Income Producing Property

The state has an interest in the applicant offsetting the state's obligation to pay for care by increasing the amount of income the applicant has available to pay for his or her care. Medicaid recognizes that a person may have property that generates income and wants to encourage the use of that property so as to perpetuate the flow of income and the ability of the applicant to provide maintenance and self-support. Examples of income producing property include agriculture interests, a retail store, and even rental investment property. When evaluating the legitimacy of the income producing property, including rental property, look to see if the property is producing income consistent with its value. The applicant does not need to be the sole owner of the property. He or she may own only a partial interest in the property.

Life Estates

Still another way to protect assets is the purchase of a life estate in real property. A life estate is an interest in real property that gives the life estate holder the right to live, enjoy, rent or otherwise use the property as his or her own during that person's life. The purchase of the life estate is not a transfer so long as it is for fair market value. The fair market value is determined by adjusting the value of the interest in the property purchased by factoring in the life expectancy of the purchaser of the life estate. The older the person is the lower the value of the life estate interest. The interesting twist here is that the value of the life estate after purchase is effectively treated as zero by Medicaid. If the life estate is subsequently transferred there is no penalty assessed against the applicant since the value of the life estate used to calculate the penalty is zero.

Jargon Cutter. The term "life estate" refers to a type of ownership in real property where the ownership interest is split in two. One interest is the remainder interest that represents a future right to own all the property, and the other, a life estate which is the right to live and enjoy the property as an owner. However, that right expires when the life estate holder dies. Upon that event the remainder interest turns into a full owner

Recent changes in the law contained within the Deficit Reduction Act have drastically restricted the use of this technique by requiring the purchaser to live in the house for at least a year prior to application for benefits in order to make the purchase a non-disqualifying transfer.

Life Insurance

While the purchase of life insurance to protect assets is not a strategy to preserve an applicant's assets, the ownership of life insurance does factor in the overall determination of eligibility for benefits. Life insurance can be counted as part of the applicant's allowed assets. Generally speaking, if the total face value of all the policies owned by the applicant are more than $2,500 then the cash value of the polices is counted as an asset. However, should the face value of the policy be less than $2,500 then the cash value will not be counted a part of the applicant's allowable assets. If there is countable cash value, then in order to become eligible, the cash value must be reduced by either taking a loan against the policy, or taking the cash out completely by surrendering the policy.

Jargon Cutter. When evaluating life insurance it is important to know the distinction between whole life policies and term policies. Generally whole life policies have a cash value that will be counted as an asset, term policies do not. Most policies that are or were paid for by an employer are group term policies and have no cash value.

Recent "creative" insurance policies that have no cash value but pay out an income stream after the insured's death, also known as reversionary annuities, have been determined by Medicaid to be a transfer of assets. Medicaid views this particular type of an insurance policy as providing no value to the applicant, essentially making the purchase of this insurance product a disqualifying transfer.

Loans and Promissory Notes

Loans and promissory notes have been the subject of much discussion and inspection by Medicaid over the years. You may find varying interpretations across jurisdictions. Currently in Florida, if the loan was made before March 1, 2005, and it cannot be converted to cash by selling or assigning it, then it will have no value as an asset, but the payments being made will be considered income to the applicant. If the loan was made after March 1, 2005, then the total amount still due under the note will be counted as an asset. You should read that sentence again. The entire balance left to be paid will be the value counted as the applicant's asset and will potentially disqualify the applicant from benefits.

Annuities

Another category of preservation strategies attempts to use investments called annuities to convert assets into income thereby reducing the amount of countable assets of the applicant. After the implementation of the Deficit Reduction Act, I do not recommend the use of annuities to qualify for Medicaid benefits. The annuity strategy is supposed to work by changing the asset into an income stream removing the assets from being counted against the applicant, however, under the new rules the purchase of an annuity may now be considered a disqualifying transfer.

The annuity strategy represents perhaps the most significant potential danger for disqualification of all the possible strategies. If the annuity is not written with the correct terms, and if the applicant's situation is not just right, the use of an annuity can do more harm than good. After the annuity is purchased it is an irrevocable act and cannot be undone. Under the Deficit Reduction Act enacted February 8, 2006, and implemented in Florida on November 1, 2007, annuities and their use in Medicaid planning have been severely restricted or eliminated.
The new law effectively eliminates the use of the annuity as a planning opportunity by requiring that the State be made the beneficiary of the annuity after the applicant dies. This requirement makes the use of annuities much, much less attractive.

Please exercise extreme caution if you are considering an annuity to qualify for Medicaid benefits. Many annuity salesmen may not be aware of the recent changes in the law. If they are telling you that an annuity is the way to Medicaid qualification, ask them what they know about the Deficit Reduction Act of 2005. If they say they never heard of it, run in the other direction as fast as you can.

Watch out! Any annuity purchased after the implementation of the Deficit Reduction Act requires the state to be the beneficiary in first position for single applicants and in second position if there is a spouse.

In recent years there has been a marked increase in the number and aggressiveness of insurance agents and brokers hawking annuities as the path to Medicaid qualification. It is my opinion that this creates an abuse of the annuity as a potential path to application. In most cases the annuity strategy is not a choice for asset preservation.

The annuity is like a surgeon's scalpel, a tool that should not be wielded by untrained hands. Even scarier, in light of the new federal legislation, the use of annuities in Medicaid planning will henceforth actually result in a denial of eligibility in most cases. Many insurance sales people are not aware of the changes to the law and continue to sell annuities as a valid Medicaid planning solution. Since the annuity purchase is an irrevocable act, the person is disqualified without any solution to unwind the annuity to fix the problem, resulting in an absolute disqualification of Medicaid benefits.

Again, annuities are a problematic solution. They have in the past offered a readily available and relatively easy solution to asset preservation and Medicaid qualification. However, they fell out of favor after the implementation of the Deficit Reduction Act (DRA). Annuities in themselves are not bad, using them to qualify for Medicaid, though, is usually not a good idea due to their severe limitations and beneficiary designation requirements under the new DRA rules.

The new annuity rules really break the annuity as a Medicaid planning solution. These rules require that the state be made the beneficiary of the annuity so that after the applicant/annuitant dies the remaining proceeds of the annuity go to the state. It is hard for me to understand where the benefit to the applicant/recipient is in this situation, especially in light of the other planning techniques that allow for the preservation of the assets for the family after the death of the Medicaid recipient.

Reality Check. Annuities can backfire on you in other ways as well. For example, in one of my cases, a wife placed her husband in a nursing home. His income was $1,500 per month, her income was $1,300. On the advice of an insurance broker she purchased a "Medicaid friendly" annuity with her excess assets in the amount of $60,000. The broker promised that the assets would not be touched by Medicaid. The annuity paid her about $500 each month for the next 120 months.

A spouse is often able to divert to herself some of the applicant's income. This is known as a spousal diversion. But in this case, the income from the annuity increased her monthly income, thereby reducing, dollar for dollar, the amount that could have been diverted to her from her husband's income. Her husband qualified for Medicaid but she lost $500 in income due to the loss of her right to receive some of her husband's income. In this situation she effectively preserved none of her assets.

Personal Care Contracts

One asset protection strategy that has come into use in some jurisdictions is the use of personal care contracts, sometimes referred to as support and maintenance agreements. The assets of the prospective Medicaid applicant are used to pay in advance for care and support, effectively moving the asset out of the applicant's ownership.

The prospective applicant can pay a family member to provide additional services that the nursing home does not usually provide. These personal care services are a legitimate expense. It does not matter whether or not they are provided by a family member or an independent party. As long as the value of the services are equal to, or greater than the amount paid for them, it is not considered a disqualifying gift.

This strategy will most often entail the use of a contract between the family member and the applicant that describes exactly what services are to be rendered, for how long, and for what compensation. The interesting part of this strategy is that the provider of the services can be a family member. The key here is that you are using the assets to pay for services. Your are not giving the assets away. Since no assets are being given away, there is no transfer for less than fair market value, and therefore no penalty. The services being provided must not be duplicative of what is covered by Medicaid. The services are usually provided for the life expectancy of the applicant. It is usually a good idea to keep a record of the times and services provided. Additional consideration must be made concerning how to treat the payment for the services for income tax purposes.

Spousal Refusal

Back in the 80's Nancy Reagan coined a phrase "Just say no." related to the war on drugs. This phrase has now come to represent one of the most emotionally charged yet singularly simplistic strategies used to qualify for Medicaid benefits.

In some jurisdictions, one spouse cannot be made responsible for the nursing home bill of the other. Yes, you married to death do you part, in sickness and in health, but nowhere in the vows or in the law of Medicaid are you required to pay the nursing home bill of your spouse.

While the assets of a married couple are effectively counted together when determining eligibility, by changing the ownership of the assets into the name of the non- applying spouse, and then having the non-applying spouse affirmatively refuse to make the assets available, or just say no to being responsible to pay the nursing home, the other spouse may become eligible for benefits.

This spousal refusal strategy works on the theory that the recalcitrant or uncooperative spouse should not be able to, by his or her inaction, keep the other spouse from accessing benefits. As strange as it may seem this actually works, but of all the strategies we use to help our clients this seemingly simple strategy is the least popular and most often rejected option. Many clients seem to equate saying no to abandoning their spouse. Emotionally, this strategy is often too hard for many to embrace.

Like so many things in the world of Medicaid, timing and sequence of implementation are absolutely imperative in order to obtain a positive result. One common mistake is to make a transfer of assets to the non-applying spouse after the non-applying spouse signs the spousal refusal forms. This has been held to be a transfer of assets and results in disqualification. A further downside of this strategy is that the non-applying spouse will not be eligible to receive any of the applicant's income under a spousal allotment or diversion.

Hardship

The transfer of assets or other disqualifying act can be ignored by the state if you are able to prove that there is a hardship. A hardship is defined as a situation that would place the applicant's life at risk because of being disqualified for benefits. In practice though, it is rare if ever, that an applicant is successful in a request for a hardship exception. After the introduction of the new stricter and senior unfriendly rules in the Deficit Reduction Act, Congress emphasized that if these new rules would act to endanger the life of the individual then a hardship exception could be used to allow qualification for Medicaid benefits. It was almost as if Congress was saying that the new rules were so bad and potentially so harmful, that they needed some way to make it okay.

Pooled Trusts

Pooled trusts are an interesting planning concept that allows for the transfer of assets without penalty, to a trust established to provide extra care for the individual in the nursing home. In the right cases this may be an effective way to use the applicant's assets to continue to supplement the care he or she is receiving in the nursing home.

Pooled trusts, also known as d4C trusts after the provision within the federal law at 42 USC 1396 p (d)(4)(C) states the requirements for a pooled trust. Pooled trusts present a planning opportunity where an unlimited amount of assets can be transferred to the pooled trust. The assets are then able to be used for the benefit of the applicant. The transfer does not create any disqualification and the assets in the trust are exempt from being counted. Any distribution made out of the trust for the benefit of the applicant is not considered income to the applicant. The funds in the trust can be used for anything so long as it benefits the applicant.

The pooled trust is a unique solution with some unique features. First the trust is not created by the applicant, but instead usually already exists and is joined by applicant. Pooled trusts are established by non-profit organizations to hold and manage the funds of many individuals. The applicant joins the trust by signing a joinder agreement. The joinder agreement can be signed by the individual, parent, grandparent, court, guardian or power of attorney. The one catch here is that any unused funds remaining unspent at the death of the applicant are usually retained by the trust for the other pooled trust participants.

Other State Specific Options

As stated elsewhere in this book, each state's law differs in its interpretation and implementation of Medicaid law. Confer with a local elder law attorney in your jurisdiction to see what other options may exist to help obtain Medicaid benefits.

CHAPTER **8**
MEDICAID ESTATE RECOVERY - PAYING IT BACK

●●

In this chapter:

What the state can take.

Change the estate plan or lose benefits.

The elective share question.

●●

A common misconception I frequently run across is that Medicaid will take your assets if you go into a nursing home. This is not true. As we have seen, your assets are not taken by Medicaid, they are instead counted in order to determine eligibility for benefits. Medicaid can only take or recover assets after the Medicaid recipient dies. This is known as Medicaid estate recovery.

Under Federal law the states are required to implement systems to recover what was spent by the state on the Medicaid beneficiary's care. When a Medicaid beneficiary dies, the state has an enforceable debt against the estate of the Medicaid beneficiary. Basically, the state tries to get back what it has paid to take care of the person in the nursing home from the beneficiary's assets after the person has died.

What the state can attach.

When the person dies, if Medicaid has paid for the person's care, Medicaid wants to get paid back. But paid back from what? To become eligible for Medicaid the recipient's assets were depleted or repositioned and there is usually little or nothing for the state to recover against. In essence, when the Medicaid recipient dies, his or her estate has already been moved or spent, so there is typically nothing to recover against.

In some circumstances and in some states, however, there may be something to attach. The three most common assets in jeopardy are the home, business property, and personal injury settlements. Of these, protecting the home from recovery is the primary and most common concern to most people.

The law regarding recovery of assets from a Medicaid beneficiary is very state specific. Every state has different rules as to what is and is not recoverable from the Medicaid beneficiary's estate. It is extremely important to determine how your state handles recovery from the Medicaid beneficiary's estate in order to properly plan to protect any assets that would be at risk of loss to Medicaid.

After the Medicaid beneficiary dies, the home may be lost to the state in order to pay the state back for the care provided by Medicaid. I say MAY be lost since each state applies a different approach to the home after the Medicaid beneficiaries death as well as whether or not you have taken steps to insulate the home from recovery.

The home, while not counted as an asset when determining eligibility, is in nearly every state, an asset available to pay back Medicaid after the applicant's death. Florida is an exception. Florida has its own set of unique rules and policies concerning paying back Medicaid. The home in Florida cannot be taken by Medicaid so long as it was the homestead of the person who died. If the property was the primary residence of the Medicaid beneficiary and it is being distributed to a blood relative, it should be considered homestead. This invaluable protection afforded to the Florida homestead can be placed at risk in several different ways. One common mistake in Florida, is to put a direction in the will of the Medicaid beneficiary to sell the home and distribute the proceeds, another is to give the home to a non-family member. Both mistakes will cause the home to be lost to Medicaid. Florida residents need to pay close attention to who and to where the home goes after the death of the Medicaid beneficiary or risk losing the home to the state.

In states other than Florida, where the post death homestead protection does not exist, you must pay even closer attention to the ownership and distribution of the home to avoid it being lost after the death of the Medicaid beneficiary.

Jargon Cutter. The term "homestead" can be confusing to many clients. There are tax definitions, and probate definitions, and Medicaid definitions. In the context of Medicaid planning, homestead refers to the primary residence of the applicant or spouse. This special status makes the home a non-countable asset during application. It can also extend to a home in a different state than the state where Medicaid is being applied for depending on whether or not the two states have a reciprocal agreement not to count the other state's homestead. Some states will confer special status to the home after death to protect it from creditors if it is the person's homestead.

Safeguarding assets other than the home from Medicaid estate recovery requires additional attention. In some cases a change of estate plan from a will to a trust can protect the assets from recovery. In Florida, if the assets pass to the beneficiaries from the revocable living trust instead of through the will and probate process, those assets will be protected from recovery. **Change the estate plan or lose benefits.**

One very common and fatal mistake in Medicaid planning is to ignore the estate plan of the healthy spouse. Failure to modify the estate plan of the applicant's spouse is often overlooked during the Medicaid planning process. There is such a focus on obtaining benefits and protecting assets that the possibility of the healthy spouse dying first is overlooked. Most spouses have reciprocal estate plans that give everything to the surviving spouse when the first spouse dies. Upon the death of the spouse the Medicaid beneficiary's asset eligibility amount is reduced from the combined $111,560 to $2,000. If the estate plan is not corrected, the death of the community spouse and the passing of assets to the Medicaid beneficiary will destroy his or her eligibility for Medicaid.

When a healthy husband and a wife set up their estate plan and the nursing home is the last thing on anyone's mind, the plan usually states that when one spouse dies all of his or her assets will go to the surviving spouse. These reciprocal estate plans are ticking time bombs waiting to destroy Medicaid eligibility. In nearly every husband and wife case the will or other estate plan of the community spouse must be changed to make sure all the couple's assets will not be distributed to the spouse who is in need of Medicaid benefits. The plan must direct that the assets go to a trust for the benefit of the surviving spouse or to family members other than the surviving spouse in order to preserve Medicaid eligibility. We typically use a specific trust mandated by the Medicaid rules called a Special Needs Trust to take the place of the Medicaid recipient. The assets that go into this trust are available to be used for the benefit of the Medicaid recipient, but do not count as his or her assets and therefore do not disqualify the spouse from continuing to receive benefits.

In a recent presentation I gave to a group of Alzheimer's caregivers in central Florida an informal poll showed that most had not made any plans to deal with the caregiver's premature death. There was a collected exclamation upon their simultaneous realization that such an obvious problem had gone unnoticed and unsolved.

In some cases the pending death of a spouse can be used to move assets to trigger eligibility of the surviving spouse. On more than one occasion we have taken the unfortunate luck of one spouse and used judicious estate planning to trigger immediate eligibility upon his or her death for the survivor.

Reality Check. In several cases over the last few years we have come upon the following situation: One spouse has a terminal illness that is progressing rapidly towards its inevitable conclusion, the other spouse has been cared for by the terminal spouse because of cognitive issues related to Alzheimer's. The loss of the terminal caregiver will present many challenges for the family, not the least of which is the issue of care and how that care will be provided. If the nursing home is going to be the answer by modifying the estate plan along with a movement of all the assets into the ownership of the terminal spouse prior to death, we can trigger Medicaid eligibility immediately upon the death of the terminal caregiver.

The elective share dilemma.

It is very important to know how your state deals with the issues of estate recovery. Recent rule changes have threatened to complicate the situation. In Florida, for example, the Department of Children and Families (DCF) has recently threatened to make policy changes regarding continuing eligibility of Nursing Home Institutional Care Program Medicaid (ICP) recipients. The Problem: When one spouse is on Medicaid in a nursing home, and the spouse who is still at home dies, the spouse in the nursing home may lose his or her eligibility for Medicaid even if the well spouse changed his or her will to bypass the ill spouse and distribute the assets elsewhere.

For example, Susan and Sam are married. Sam has been in a nursing home for the last year. Early in his placement he applied for and was approved for Medicaid. At the time of application, the wife took steps to change her will so all her assets, totaling $90,000, go to her children instead of her husband. Then, unexpectedly, Susan dies. What effect, if any, does her death have on her surviving husband's continuing eligibility for Medicaid benefits?

The rules specifically exempt from penalty transfers made through a will due to the death of the spouse. The husband's asset level was not increased since the wife's assets went by her will to the children and not her husband. The husband could be disqualified from Medicaid however should a policy be enforced stating the Medicaid recipient must apply for all benefits they are entitled to, It has been proposed that this may mean taking 30 percent of his deceased wife's estate. This 30 percent share is known as the elective share.

The surviving spouse is entitled, under many state elective share laws, to "elect" or take 30 percent of their deceased spouse's estate.

Jargon Cutter. "Elective share" is that amount to which a disinherited or under inherited spouse is entitled to from deceased spouses estate. It is usually set at 30 percent of the value of the spouse's estate. It's purpose is to keep one spouse from disinheriting the other.

The total estate of the deceased spouse, including amounts in a living trust, amounts in joint accounts, and amounts in life insurance can be considered when calculating the 30 percent share. If the Medicaid applicant does not make the election, then he or she could be considered to have failed to apply for benefits to which he or she was otherwise entitled. This failure to apply may disqualify the surviving spouse from Medicaid.

The repercussions of Medicaid disqualification because of the elective share issue are wide and far reaching. First, the nursing home no longer has a payment source for the care they are providing. If Medicaid is not paying the nursing home and there is no community spouse to make payment, who is going to pay the facility? Where is the nursing home resident going to go if he or she is discharged for failure to pay? To make matters worse, what happens if he or she is not able to make the election because he or she is incapacitated, infirm or without the financial resources to go forward with the election? To compound the situation, the nursing home may not find out about the disqualification until many months after the death of the spouse when the surviving spouse's case comes up for annual review by Medicaid. It is not clear whether the facility may have to pay back monies erroneously received.

For the unprepared, a world of uncertainty can await. At the present time, Florida Medicaid is not requiring that the elective share be made. Florida policy, as of the date of this publication, regarding the elective share has flip flopped from not requiring the election, to requiring the election, to now not requiring the election. There is a solution though, that can remove the continuing ambiguity for those who take corrective measures in advance.

In the most recent modification of Florida's elective share rules, a provision was made to allow an elective share qualified special needs trust. This trust uses a will to create a testamentary trust dedicated to providing for the special needs of the surviving spouse. At least 30 percent of the decedent spouse's estate must go into the trust. By having this trust in place, the assets go to the trust, not the spouse, and the eligibility of the Medicaid recipient continues uninterrupted. It should be emphasized that Florida policy as of the date of this publication does not require the election to be made. So it would appear that this is a solution without a problem in Florida at the present time.

CHAPTER 9
CHOOSING A NURSING HOME

●●●

In this chapter:

Making the choice.

The selection factors.

Questions to ask the nursing home.

Questions to ask yourself.

Information resources.

●●●

The doctor has just told you that your husband cannot be discharged home. He needs rehab for his broken hip and will need to go to a nursing home. Or, maybe, you have been taking care of your mother for several years, but now her Alzheimer's disease has taken its toll and she needs more care than you can provide. THAT day has come. What do you do? You are now faced with the moment when the nursing home switches from a possibility and becomes a reality. Where to start looking? Which one is the best? Where can you find a recommendation? Do you have to use the one the hospital recommends? Do you have a choice? What are you going to do now?

Making the choice

First thing, take a deep breath. There are a lot of resources out there to help clear away some of the confusion. There are many resources from both state and federal agencies that can help give you insight and further guidance in making your choice if you know where to look. Many of these sites are difficult to find even with the perfect Google search. With a little guidance from the links provided below, you can be on your way to finding the best nursing homes near you. On these sites you can find detailed information including: inspection results, staffing levels, complaints, size and ownership, even whether they speak Creole. Nursinghomefinder.com is a site we have set up to help narrow the choices and make it easier for you to find a nursing home.

Choosing a nursing home is often done during a crisis. You may need a nursing home in a hurry because a loved one is about to be discharged from the hospital. This time crunch makes the selection process a lot tougher. Personal recommendations are always a good place to start. Ask your doctor, friends, and family if they have suggestions. Recommendations from the hospital social worker or discharge planner can obviously be helpful, ask for a list of facilities and a recommendation. The hospital social workers and discharge planners intend to help, however, they may inadvertently steer you to nursing homes that do not fit your circumstances or needs.

Always try to visit the nursing home first before selecting a facility. Remember, you make the decision what nursing home to use.

There are differences of opinion as to whether or not to call the facility to schedule a visit. The unannounced visit can often give you a better feel for what the facility is really like. Meal times are often the best time to see the staff in action. If there are problems this busy time can often bring the problems to the forefront. Scheduling a time with the facility though can be more efficient in that the facility can make sure they have someone available to tour you through the facility. If you have the time try to visit the facility again, but at a different time. The staffing levels often change with the time of day or on the weekends.

If you are coming out of the hospital and need extra time to find an appropriate nursing home, you can often gain a few days by appealing your hospital discharge. Rules for appealing the discharge can be found in the "Important Message from Medicare" that must be included in the hospital admission packet. The appeals process is fairly strict on the timing of the appeal. You must contact what is known as the Quality Improvement Organization (QIO) no later then the proposed date of discharge and before you leave the hospital. Once you have called the QIO your appeal has started. The Center for Medicare Advocacy also has some additional tips on discharge planning advocacy and challenging a discharge. Go to www.medicareadvocacy.org. Click on "Info by topic," then choose "Acute Hospital Care."

Selection factors

You have heard the three most important considerations in any real estate purchase is location, location and location. It is not much different in nursing home selection. The nursing home should be located close to family and friends or convenient on their everyday travels. Frequency of visitation is the single most important factor affecting the quality of care a resident will receive. Making it easier for family and friends to visit will have the biggest effect on the quality of care for that individual. The highest rated nursing home located across town is not as good a choice as the moderately rated facility a half mile from your home, or one that you drive by every day on your daily commute.

Special needs of the resident must be addressed. Is there a need for some form of specialty care? For example, if you are looking to place a person who has Alzheimer's disease, the ability of the facility to provide a secure, locked area, with specifically trained staff would be a critical selection factor. Specialized wound care and ventilator care are other issues to consider.

Inspection reports can provide you great insight into the inner workings of a nursing home and the quality of care. Every nursing home that accepts Medicaid or Medicare is supposed to be inspected once a year. They must have the results of those inspections available for your review upon request. If you are too shy to ask for the reports you can get them online at www. medicare.gov.

Watch out! Claims of specialty care made by the nursing home can be misleading. Dementia care for example can mean a lot of different things.

Look under the "search tools" section and choose "nursing home compare." Few nursing homes have a perfect record. When reviewing the reports if you see a problem, keep in mind that while the problem may indicate an issue, more important though, is what the facility plans to do or did to correct the problem. Ask the facility about the issue. How did they resolve it?

Questions to ask the nursing home

- Do they accept Medicare and Medicaid as payment sources.
- Are they a rehab only facility or do they provide long-term custodial care?
- What is the daily basic private rate?
- What type of services are not covered in the base rate?
- Are they taking new patients, if not is there a waiting list?
- Does the nursing home have any specialty care units, such as an Alzheimer's or memory care unit?
- What personal choices can the resident make, such as when

meals are scheduled, and sleep and wake times?
- Can the residents bring their own furniture or decorations?
- What kind of activities are planned on a daily basis?
- How many volunteers work in the facility?
- Are pets allowed to be brought in to visit?
- Is there an outdoor area for the residents to use?
- Do they have a copy of their most recent state survey? Ask to see it.
- Does the nursing home have any deficiencies on their last survey and what are they doing to resolve the problems?
- Can the resident continue to use their existing physician?
- Is there a resident and family council, if so, can you sit in on a meeting?
- What is the procedure for scheduling a care plan meeting?
- What is the patient to staff ratio?
- Do the residents have a choice of different foods at mealtimes?
- Do the residents have access to snacks between meals?
- Does the nursing home have a disaster plan to move the residents in the event of an emergency, and can you see it?
- How much does the facility rely on temporary staffing for coverage on weekends and evenings?
- What is the procedure in the event of a emergency with the resident?
- How can you contact the facility in the event of an emergency?

Questions to ask yourself

- Does the nursing home meet your personal and cultural needs?
- Is there a perceptible odor of urine?
- How well does it appear that the staff and the residents interact?
- Does the food smell and look good?
- Are the hallways clear of clutter?
- Is the lighting good?
- What is the overall attitude of the nursing home's staff?
- What type of residents are in the particular home? Are they alert or not?

Key Point. Make sure that the nursing home you are considering accepts the method of payment you will be using. While most nursing homes accept Medicaid, not all do. Also if you have a Medicare Advantage Plan, double check with your plan to see if the facility you want is on their provider list.

Resource List

The following resources and links will help in the quest for care and alternatives and includes resources for the caregiver as well.

The Nursing Home Guide - www.ahcaxnet.fdhc.state.fl.us/ nhcguide - This Florida state specific guide gives detailed information on all the nursing homes in Florida. It includes a star rating system to help summarize the facilities' qualifications. To receive the guide by mail, call AHCA toll-free at (888) 419-3456 or write to:

Agency for Health Care Administration Bureau of Field
Operations/CAU, MS #49
2727 Mahan Drive
Tallahassee, FL 32308

Check with your state's agency for health care administration for similar guides.

Nursing Home Compare - www.medicare.gov - Click on "Compare Nursing Homes in Your Area" to narrow the search area. There is a wealth of information here, almost to the point of overload. This site contains information on every nursing home in the United States. This guide is available only online.

Florida Health Finder - www.facilitylocator.floridahealthstat.com - Presents a comprehensive resource to locate any type of health care provider including nursing homes in the state of Florida.

Florida Department of Elder Affairs - www.floridaelderresource. com - This is yet another directory listing for health care providers including nursing homes and assisted living facilities.

Alzheimer's Disease Education and Referral Center - www. alzheimers.nia.nih.gov -This is a service of the National Institute on Aging. It presents information and additional resources on diagnosis, treatment, patient care, caregiver needs, long-term care, education and training related to Alzheimer's Disease.

Alzheimer's Disease Education and Referral Center
P.O. Box 8250
Silver Springs, MD 20907-8250
800-438-4380
adear@nia.nih.gov

Children of Aging Parents - www.caps4caregivers.org is a nonprofit group that provides information and materials for adult children caring for their older parents.

Children of Aging Parents
P.O. Box 167
Richboro, PA 18954
800-227-7294

Eldercare Locator - www.eldercare.gov or 800-677-1116 is a nationwide service designed to help older people and caregivers locate local support and resources.

Family Caregiver Alliance - www.caregiver.org is a community based nonprofit organization providing support services and additional information for those caring for people with Alzheimer's Disease, stroke, traumatic brain injury and other cognitive disorders.

Family Caregiving 101 - www.familycaregiving101.org provides materials and insight to assist the caregiver. This is a good starting point with straightforward easily accessible information.

The National Institute on Aging Information Center - www.nia.hih.gov is the federal government's main web site for all things age related. You can order publications, sign up for e-mail alerts and link to other federal resources including NIHSeniorHealth.gov. This site has special features to make the text larger or have it read aloud.

The Simon Foundation for Continence - www.simonfoundation.org helps individuals with the challenges of incontinence. The foundation provides books, tapes, pamphlets and other resources. Incontinency is one of the chief contributing factors in nursing home placement. Successful management or treatment can often delay placement.

Well Spouse Association - www.wellspouse.org is a nonprofit membership organization that provides support for wives, husbands, and partners of chronically ill and or disabled individuals. They also publish the bimonthly newsletter, *Mainstay*.

Videocaregiving - videocaregiving.org is perhaps one of my favorite sites about caregiving. Its insightful and well produced short films put a face on caregiving and provide real world solutions and insight into the demands of caregiving.

CHAPTER 10
CONCLUSION - THE GOOD NEWS

It is my hope that by the time you reach this part of the book you have a better understanding of Medicaid and how it works to pay for the costs of a nursing home. You should know how Medicaid eligibility is determined, what is counted and what is not and lastly, you should have some insight to what can be done to become eligible for benefits.

Medicaid is a complex and convoluted system that is ever changing and even though the Medicaid program seems to have strict financial requirements, the reader should now realize that there are options that can enable a family to qualify for benefits. Qualification preserves a large part, if not all, of the assets for the remaining family members as well as the person in the nursing home. Planning to protect assets and obtain benefits for long-term care takes careful consideration of the entire financial and legal picture of the applicant and spouse.

The law of Medicaid continues to evolve. The most recent changes to Medicaid in DRA 2005 put seniors and their families even more at risk of financial catastrophe. The changes to the transfer rules and the start date for disqualification penalties have the potential to disqualify every applicant from receiving Medicaid benefits. We have already seen some nursing homes reject placement of potential residents simply because they reported making gifts in the last five years. At no time in the history of Medicaid is it more important to have competent guidance through this ever changing area of the law.

Failure to plan will result in requiring that the assets be spent on nursing home bills until the asset eligibility levels are eventually reached. With proper planning the spouse can keep the necessary funds to maintain a quality lifestyle, maintain the potential inheritance for the family, and have assets left to augment the care of the person in the nursing home. For more information on Medicaid and other legal issues affecting seniors and to update the information contained within this book, be sure to check our web site at www.virtuallawoffice.com.

APPENDIX

●●●

This appendix is provided to help you localize the information in this book to your particular state's jurisdiction. Every effort has been made to assure its accuracy, however, you MUST confer with a local elder law attorney for current and up-to-date information. These numbers change often. Please do not rely on them in making any determination regarding Medicaid eligibility. For a list of elder law attorneys in your state please visit www.virtuallawoffice.com.

APPENDIX A - 2010 MONTHLY PERSONAL NEEDS ALLOWANCE

STATE	BENEFIT	STATE	NEEDS BENEFIT
Alabama	$30.00	Montana	$50.00
Alaska	$75.00	Nebraska	$50.00
Arizona	$101.10	Nevada	$35.00
Arkansas	$40.00	New Hampshire	$56.00
California	$35.00	New Jersey	$35.00
Colorado	$50.00	New Mexico	$63.00
Connecticut	$69.00	New York	$50.00
Delaware	$44.00	North Carolina	$30.00
District of Columbia	$70.00	North Dakota	$50.00
Florida	$35.00	Ohio	$40.00
Georgia	$50.00	Oklahoma	$50.00
Hawaii	$50.00	Oregon	$30.00
Idaho	$40.00	Pennsylvania	$45.00
Illinois	$30.00	Rhode Island	$50.00
Indiana	$52.00	South Carolina	$30.00
Iowa	$50.00	South Dakota	$60.00
Kansas	$60.00	Tennessee	$50.00
Kentucky	$40.00	Texas	$60.00

Louisiana	$38.00	Utah	$45.00
Maine	$40.00	Vermont	$47.66
Maryland	$71.00	Virginia	$40.00
Massachusetts	$72.80	Washington	$57.28
Michigan	$60.00	West Virginia	$50.00
Minnesota	$89.00	Wisconsin	$45.00
Mississippi	$44.00	Wyoming	$50.00
Missouri	$30.00		

APPENDIX B - 2010 MONTHLY PENALTY DIVISOR

STATE	DIVISOR	STATE	DIVISOR
Alabama	$4,800.00	New Hampshire	$262.99 - Per Day, $7,889.70 - Per Month
Alaska	Varies	New Jersey	$7,411.80
Arizona	Maricopa, Pima and Pinal County: $5,942.65 All other Counties: $5,321.94	New Mexico	$5,269.00
Arkansas	$4,514.00	New York	Central $7,264.00
California	$6,311.00		Long Island $11,227.00
Colorado	$6,267.00		New York City $10,285.00
Connecticut	$10,366.00		Northeastern $7,927.00
Delaware	$195.35 per day, $5,860.50 per month		Northern Metropolitan $10,163.00
District of Columbia	$7,149.00		Rochester $9,058.00
Florida	$5,000.00		Western $7,694.00
Georgia	$4,916.55	North Carolina	$5,000.00
Hawaii	$8,850.00	North Dakota	$195.55 Per Day, $5,866.50 Per Month
Idaho	$200.00 per day, $6,000.00 per month	Ohio	$6,023.00

Illinois	Monthly Private Pay Rate	Oklahoma	$132.85 per day
Indiana	$4,826.00	Oregon	$6,494.00
Iowa	$159.30 per day; $4,779.00 per month	Pennsylvania	$247.06 per day; $7,235.82 per month
Kansas	$138.41 per day	Rhode Island	$7,777.00
Kentucky	$177.05 per day	South Carolina	$5,379.80
Louisiana	$4,000.00	South Dakota	$4,895.40
Maine	$7,258.00	Tennessee	$3,874.00
Maryland	$233.00 per day	Texas	$130.88 per day
Massachusetts	$274.00 per day	Utah	$4,526.00
Michigan	$6,618.00	Vermont	$218.06 per day, $6,541.80 per month
Minnesota	$5,372.00	Virginia	Northern Virginia: $6,654.00, All other: $4,954.00
Mississippi	$4,600.00	Washington	$227.00 Per Day, $6,810.00 Per Month
Missouri	$3,960.00	West Virginia	$5,087.00
Montana	$5,376.50	Wisconsin	$204.35 per day; $6,259.00 per month
Nebraska	Varies	Wyoming	$6,023.00
Nevada	$5,865.00		

APPENDIX C - MONTHLY MAINTENANCE NEEDS ALLOWANCE

STATE	ALLOWANCE		STATE	ALLOWANCE
*Alabama	$1,822.00		Montana	$1,823.00 - $2,739.00
*Alaska	$2,739.00		Nebraska	$1823.00 - $2,610.00
*Arizona	$1,822.00 - $2,739.00		*Nevada	$1,821.25 - $2,739.00
*Arkansas	$1,822.00 - $2,739.00		New Hampshire	$1,822.00 - $2,739.00
California	$2,739.00		New Jersey	$1,821.25 - $2,739.00
*Colorado	$1,822.00 - $2,739.00		*New Mexico	$1,822.00 - $2,739.00
Connecticut	$1,821.25 - $2,739.00		New York	$2,739.00
*Delaware	$1,821.25 - $2,739.00		North Carolina	$1,822.00 - $2,739.00
Dist. of Columbia	$2,739.00		North Dakota	$2,739.00
*Florida	$1,822.00 - $2,739.00		Ohio	$1,822.00 - $2,739.00
*Georgia	$2,739.00		*Oklahoma	$2,739.00
Hawaii	$2,739.00		*Oregon	$1,822.00 - $2,739.00
*Idaho	$1,822.00 - $2,739.00		Pennsylvania	$1,822.00 - $2,739.00
Illinois	$2,739.00		Rhode Island	$1,821.25 - $2,739.00
Indiana	$1,823.00 - $2,739.00		*South Carolina	$2,739.00
*Iowa	$2,739.00		*South Dakota	$1,821.25 - $2,739.00
Kansas	$1,822.00 - $2,739.00		Tennessee	$1,822.00 - $2,739.00

*Kentucky	$1,821.25- $2,739.00		*Texas	$2,739.00
*Louisiana	$2,739.00		Utah	$1,822.00 - $2,739.00
Maine	$1,822.00 - $2,739.00		Vermont	$1829.00 - $2,739.00
Maryland	$1,821.00 - $2,739.00		Virginia	$1,821.25 - $2,739.00
Massachusetts	$1,822.00 - $2,739.00		Washington	$1,822.00 - $2,739.00
Michigan	$1,821.25 - $2,739.00		West Virginia	$1,822.00 - $2,739.00
Minnesota	$1,823.00 - $2,739.00		Wisconsin	$2,428.33 - $2,739.00
*Mississippi	$2,739.00		*Wyoming	$2,739.00
Missouri	$1,822.00 - $2,739.00			

APPENDIX D - 2010 SHELTER AND UTILITY ALLOWANCE

STATE	UTILITY	SHELTER
Alabama	None	None
Alaska	None	None
Arizona	$326	$525
Arkansas	$247	$525
California	None	None
Colorado	$418	$525
Connecticut	$720	$525
Delaware	$440 with heat $302 without heat	$526
Dist. of Columbia	$276	None
Florida	$198	$525
Georgia	None	None
Hawaii	None	None
Idaho	$400	$525
Illinois	None	None
Indiana	$429	$525
Iowa	None	None
Kansas	$334	$446
Kentucky	Uses Actual	$525
Louisiana	None	None
Maine	$700	$525
Maryland	$224 with heat, $371 without heat	$525
Massachusetts	$612 with heat, $375 without heat	$525
Michigan	$550	$525
Minnesota	$305 with heat, $75 without heat, phone $24	$526
Mississippi	None	None

Missouri	$262	$525
Montana	$534	$526
Nebraska	$312	$525
Nevada	$274	$525
New Hampshire	$584	$525
New Jersey	$411 with heat, $251 without heat, phone $29	$525
New Mexico	$278 with heat, $101 without heat, phone $32	$525
New York	None	None
North Carolina	$266	$525
North Dakota	None	None
Ohio	$586	$525
Oklahoma	None	None
Oregon	$379 with heat, $262 without heat	$525
Pennsylvania	$491.00 with heat, $258.00 without heat, phone $32.00	$525
Rhode Island	$556	$525
South Carolina	None	None
South Dakota	$645	$525
Tennessee	$293	$525
Texas	None	None
Utah	$257	$525
Vermont	$744	$549
Virginia	$290	$525
Washington	$384	$525
West Virginia	$366	$525
Wisconsin	$305 with heat, $208 without heat, phone $29.00	$700
Wyoming	None	None

APPENDIX E - 2010 NON-COUNTABLE RESOURCE EXEMPTION
WHOLE LIFE INSURANCE

STATE	EXEMPTION		STATE	EXEMPTION
Alabama	$5,000		Kansas	$1,500
Alaska	$1,500		Kentucky	$1,500
Arizona	$1,500		Montana	$1,500
Arkansas	$1,500		Nebraska	$1,500
California	$1,500		Nevada	$1,500
Colorado	$1,500		New Hampshire	$1,500
Connecticut	$1,500		New Jersey	$1,500
Florida	$2,500		New Mexico	$1,500
Delaware	$1,500		New York	$1,500
Dist. of Columbia	$1,500		North Carolina	$10,000
Georgia	$1,500		North Dakota	$1,500
Hawaii	$1,500		Ohio	$1,500
Idaho	$1,500		Oklahoma	$1,500
Illinois	$1,500		Oregon	$1,500
Indiana	$10,000		Pennsylvania	$1,500
Iowa	$1,500		Rhode Island	$1,500

South Carolina	$1,500		Missouri	$1,500
South Dakota	$1,500		Tennessee	$1,500
Louisiana	$10,000		Texas	$1,500
Maine	$1,500		Vermont	$1,500
Maryland	$1,500		Virginia	$1,500
Massachusetts	$1,500		Washington	$1,500
Michigan	$1,500		West Virginia	$1,500
Minnesota	$1,500		Wisconsin	$1,500
Mississippi	$10,000		Wyoming	$1,500

APPENDIX F - 2010 INDIVIDUAL COUNTABLE RESOURCE ALLOWANCE

STATE	ALLOWANCE	STATE	ALLOWANCE
Alabama	$2,000	Montana	$2,000
Alaska	$2,000	Nebraska	$4,000
Arizona	$2,000	Nevada	$2,000
Arkansas	$2,000	New Hampshire	$2,500
California	$2,000	New Jersey	$2,000
Colorado	$2,000	New Mexico	$2,000
Connecticut	$1,600	New York	$13,800
Delaware	$2,000	North Carolina	$2,000
District of Columbia	$4,000	North Dakota	$3,000
Florida	$2,000	Ohio	$1,500
Georgia	$2,000	Oklahoma	$2,000
Hawaii	$2,000	Oregon	$2,000
Idaho	$2,000	Pennsylvania	$2,400
Illinois	$2,000	Rhode Island	$4,000
Indiana	$1,500	South Carolina	$2,000
Iowa	$2,000	South Dakota	$2,000
Kansas	$2,000	Tennessee	$2,000

Kentucky	$2,000	Texas	$2,000
Louisiana	$2,000	Utah	$2,000
Maine	$10,000	Vermont	$2,000
Maryland	$2,500	Virginia	$2,000
Massachusetts	$2,000	Washington	$2,000
Michigan	$2,000	West Virginia	$2,000
Minnesota	$3,000	Wisconsin	$2,000
Mississippi	$4,000	Wyoming	$2,000
Missouri	$999.99		

APPENDIX G - 2010 COMMUNITY SPOUSE COUNTABLE RESOURCE ALLOWANCE

STATE	ALLOWANCE	STATE	ALLOWANCE
Alabama	$25,000 - $109,560	Montana	$21,912 - $109,560
Alaska	$109,560	Nebraska	$21,912 - $109,560
Arizona	$21,912 - $109,560	Nevada	$21,912 - $109,560
Arkansas	$21,912 - $109,560	New Hampshire	$21,912 - $109,560
California	$109,560	New Jersey	$21,912 - $109,560
Colorado	$109,560	New Mexico	$31,290 - $109,560
Connecticut	$21,912 - $109,560	New York	$74,820 - $109,560
Delaware	$25,000 - $109,560	North Carolina	$21,912 - $109,560
Dist. of Colubmia	$21,912 - $109,560	North Dakota	$21,912 - $109,560
Florida	$109,560	Ohio	$21,912 - $109,560
Georgia	$109,560	Oklahoma	$25,000 - $109,560
Hawaii	$109,560	Oregon	$21,912 - $109,560
Idaho	$21,912 - 109,560	Pennsylvania	$21,912 - $109,560
Illinois	$109,560	Rhode Island	$21,912 - $109,560
Indiana	$21,912 - $109,560	South Carolina	$66,480
Iowa	$24,000 - 109,560	South Dakota	$21,912 - $109,560

Kansas	$21,912 - $109,560	Tennessee	$21,912 - $109,560
Kentucky	$21,912.00 - 109,560	Texas	$21,912 - $109,560
Louisiana	$109,560	Utah	$21,912 - $109,560
Maine	$109,560	Vermont	$109,560
Maryland	$21,912 - $109,560	Virginia	$21,912 - $109,560
Massachusetts	$109,560	Washington	$48,639 - $109,560
Michigan	$21,912 - $109,560	West Virginia	$21,912 - $109,560
Minnesota	$31,094 - $109,560	Wisconsin	$50,000 - $109,560
Mississippi	$109,560	Wyoming	$109,560
Missouri	$21,912 - $109,560		

APPENDIX H - STATE CONTACT INFORMATION

State	Ombudsman	State Survey Agency	Medicaid	Health Insurance Assistance Program
Alabama	(877) 425-2243	(800) 356-9596	(800) 362-1504	(800) 243-5463
Alaska	(800) 730-6393	(888) 387-9387	(800) 780-9972	(800) 478-6065
Samoa	(888) 875-9229	(808) 692-7420	(808) 587-3521	(888) 875-9229
Arizona	(800) 432-4040	(602) 364-2690	(800) 523-0231	(800) 432-4040
Arkansas	(501) 682-2441	(800) 582-4887	(800) 482-5431	(800) 224-6330
California	(800) 231-4024	(800) 236-9747	(916) 636-1980	(800) 434-0222
Colorado	(800) 288-1376	(800) 886-7689	(800) 221-3943	(888) 696-7213
Connecticut	(860) 424-5200	(860) 509-7400	(800) 842-1508	(800) 994-9422
Delaware	(800) 223-9074	(877) 453-0012	(800) 372-2022	(800) 336-9500
Florida	(888) 831-0404	(888) 419-3456	(866) 762-2237	(800) 963-5337
Georgia	(888) 454-5826	(800) 878-6442	(866) 322-4260	(800) 669-8387
Guam	(888) 875-9229	(808) 692-7420	N/A	(671) 735-7382
Hawaii	(888) 875-9229	(808) 692-7420	(808) 587-3521	(888) 875-9229
Idaho	(877) 471-2777	(208) 334-6626	(877) 200-5441	(800) 247-4422
Illinois	(800) 252-8966	(800) 252-4343	(866) 468-7543	(800) 548-9034
Indiana	(800) 545-7763	(800) 246-8909	(800) 889-9949	(800) 452-4800
Iowa	(800) 532-3213	(877) 686-0027	(800) 338-8366	(800) 351-4664
Kansas	(877) 662-8362	(800) 432-3535	(800) 766-9012	(800) 860-5260
Kentucky	(800) 372-2973	(502) 564-7963	(800) 635-2570	(877) 293-7447
Louisiana	(800) 259-4990	(888) 810-1819	(888) 342-6207	(800) 259-5301
Maine	(800) 499-0229	(800) 383-2441	(800) 977-6740	(877) 353-3771
Maryland	(800) 243-3425	(877) 402-8219	(800) 492-5231	(800) 243-3425
Mass.	(800) 243-4636	(800) 462-5540	(800) 325-5231	(800) 243-4636
Michigan	(866) 485-9393	(800) 882-6006	(800) 642-3195	(800) 803-7174
Minnesota	(800) 657-3591	(800) 369-7994	(800) 657-3739	(800) 333-2433
Mississippi	(601) 359-4927	(800) 227-7308	(800) 421-2408	(800) 948-3090
Missouri	(800) 309-3282	(800) 392-0210	(800) 392-2161	(573) 817-8320
Montana	(800) 332-2272	(406) 444-2099	(800) 362-8312	(800) 551-3191
Nebraska	(800) 942-7830	(402) 471-3324	(800) 430-3244	(800) 234-7119

Nevada	(800) 243-3638	(800) 225-3414	(800) 992-0900	(800) 307-4444
N. Hampshire	(800) 442-5640	(800) 852-3345	(800) 852-3345	(866) 634-9412
New Jersey	(877) 582-6995	(800) 792-9770	(800) 356-1561	(800) 792-8820
New Mexico	(866) 842-9230	(800) 752-8649	(888) 997-2583	(800) 432-2080
New York	(800) 342-9871	(888) 201-4563	(800) 541-2831	(800) 701-0501
N. Carolina	(919) 733-8395	(800) 672-3071	(800) 662-7030	(800) 443-9354
North Dakota	(800) 451-8693	(701) 328-2352	(800) 755-2604	(888) 575-6611
Ohio	(800) 282-1206	(800) 342-0553	(800) 324-8680	(800) 686-1578
Oklahoma	(800) 211-2116	(800) 522-0203	(800) 522-0310	(800) 763-2828
Oregon	(800) 522-2602	(800) 232-3020	(800) 527-5772	(800) 722-4134
Pennsylvania	(717) 783-1550	(800) 254-5164	(800) 692-7462	(800) 783-7067
Puerto Rico	(800) 981-6015	(787) 721-3461	(877) 725-4300	(877) 725-4300
Rhode Island	(401) 785-3340	(401) 222-2566	(800) 984-8989	(401) 462-4444
S. Carolina	(800) 868-9095	(800) 922-6735	(888) 549-0820	(800) 868-9095
South Dakota	(866) 854-5465	(605) 773-3356	(800) 452-7691	(800) 536-8197
Tennessee	(877) 236-0013	(800) 778-4504	(866) 311-4287	(877) 801-0044
Texas	(800) 252-2412	(800) 458-9858	(877) 541-7905	(800) 252-9240
Utah	(800) 541-7735	(800) 662-4157	(800) 662-9651	(800) 541-7735
Vermont	(800) 889-2047	(802) 241-2345	(800) 250-8427	(800) 642-5119
Virgin Islands	(800) 981-6015	N/A	(877) 725-4300	(340) 772-7368
Virginia	(800) 938-8885	(800) 955-1819	(804) 786-7933	(800) 552-3402
Washington	(800) 562-6028	(800) 422-3263	(800) 562-3022	(800) 562-9600
Wash. DC	(800) 424-2277	(202) 442-5833	(888) 557-1116	(202) 739-0668
West Virginia	(304) 558-3317	(800) 442-2888	(304) 558-1700	(877) 987-4463
Wisconsin	(800) 815-0015	(800) 642-6552	(800) 362-3002	(800) 242-1060
Wyoming	(307) 322-5553	(800) 548-1367	(307) 777-7531	(800) 856-4398

State of Florida
Department of Children and Families

Charlie Crist
Governor

Robert A. Butterworth
Secretary

MEMORANDUM

Date: October 31, 2007   Transmittal #: P-07-10-0015

To: ACCESS Florida Operations Managers
            ACCESS Florida Program Offices

From: Jennifer Lange, Director, ACCESS Florida (**Signature on File**)

Subject: Implementation of the Deficit Reduction Act Asset Provisions

Effective: November 1, 2007

The purpose of this memorandum is to provide staff with information regarding changes in policy resulting from the Deficit Reduction Act of 2005 (DRA), signed into law February 8, 2006. Programs affected by this memorandum (unless otherwise noted) are Institutional Care (ICP), Institutional Hospice, Home and Community Based Services (HCBS) waiver, and Program of All-inclusive Care for the Elderly (PACE). For the purpose of this memo, these programs will be referred to as long term care programs.

POLICY CHANGES/NEW POLICIES

Below is a list of policies that changed, or new policies, followed by a discussion of the policy, implementation instructions, and attachments. The manual will be updated to reflect the policy changes or new policies in the quarterly release following implementation of this memorandum.

Transfer of Asset Processes

- Look-Back Period
- Multiple Transfers
- Begin Date for Applying Transfer Penalty Period
- Partial Month Penalty Periods

Special Asset Policies

- Annuities
- Home Equity Interest Exceeding $500,000
- Continuing Care Retirement Community Entrance Fees
- Promissory Notes, Loans and Mortgages

1317 Winewood Boulevard, Tallahassee, Florida 32399-0700

Mission: Protect the Vulnerable, Promote Strong and Economically Self-Sufficient Families, and
Advance Personal and Family Recovery and Resiliency

Implementation of the DRA Asset Provisions
Page 2

- Purchase of Life Estate Interest
- Long-Term Care Insurance Partnership Program

Undue Hardship Provision

- Undue Hardship Policy
- Undue Hardship Process

Attachments

- Evaluating Annuities Job Aid
- Letter to Annuity Issuer
- Third Party Recovery Transmittal
- Long-Term Care PPP Summary
- Notice of Resource or Income Transfer
- Rebuttal/Hardship Questionnaire
- Notice of Excess Home Equity Interest
- Waiver of Home Equity Limit Questionnaire
- Rebuttal/Undue Hardship Evaluation
- Rebuttal/Undue Hardship Evaluation Instructions
- How to Process Transfers for Waivers and Institutional Care
- How to Process Transfers for Institutional Hospice
- How to Re-convey an Asset Transfer when Successfully Rebutted
- How to Process Annuities in the FLORIDA System
- How to Process Home Equities Exceeding $500,000
- How to Process Continuing Care Retirement Community Entrance Fees

Implementation of the DRA Asset Provisions
Page 3

TRANSFER OF ASSET PROCESSES

Look Back Period

The current 36-month look-back period for transfers will increase to 60 months, beginning December 2010. The 60 month look back period will be "phased in" in one-month increments. More information regarding the 60 month look back period and how it will be "phased in" will be provided at a later date.

Cases will continue to be subject to the 36-month look-back period until phase-in of the 60-month look back period begins.

Multiple Transfers

The uncompensated value of all transfers made on or after November 1, 2007 are added together to arrive at one total value, with one penalty period assigned. Transfers made before November 1, 2007 will be evaluated using pre DRA policy.

Begin Date for Applying Transfer Penalty Period

The begin date of a penalty period for assets transferred on or after November 1, 2007 will be the later of the following dates:

- The first <u>day</u> the individual would be eligible for long term care Medicaid were it not for imposition of a transfer penalty (this includes filing an application and meeting all other program criteria for long term care Medicaid), or

- The first day of the month in which the individual transfers the assets, or

- The first day following the end of an existing penalty period.

<u>Example:</u> In November 2007, Mr. Smith made an asset transfer that would result in a penalty period. He applies for Medicaid in December 2007. The transfer penalty would start in December if he meets all factors of eligibility except for the transfer. Do not start the penalty period in November (when the transfer occurred) even if Mr. Smith was in receipt of long term care services, as he did not apply and qualify for Medicaid until December.

Once the penalty period is started, it will continue even if the individual later becomes ineligible for MI T (basic Medicaid without long-term care) coverage based on other eligibility factors, such as assets or income over the limits.

Continue to apply pre DRA policy for assets transferred prior to November 1, 2007.

Partial Month Penalty Periods

For transfers made on or after November 1, 2007, when a penalty period is imposed, the individual will be ineligible for a period rounded down to the nearest day. Based on this, the penalty period may be prorated in the last month and therefore, once the penalty period ends, the individual may be eligible for a portion of that month. To arrive at the length of time for a fractional penalty period:

- Total the amount of the uncompensated transfer.
- Divide that total by $5000.
- Multiply any fraction by 30 (regardless of how many days are in the month).
- The result is the length of the fractional penalty period.

Example: John Smith was admitted to a nursing home on January 3, 2007. He transfers $10,000 on November 15, 2007 and $8,500 on December 12, 2007 for which he receives no compensation and then applies for ICP on December 28, 2007. The total transfer is $18,500. The penalty period makes him ineligible for ICP-related benefits for a period of 3.7 months ($18,500 divided by $5000 = 3.7). To convert the fractional month to days, multiply .7 times 30 for a result of 21 days, or a total penalty period of 3 months and 21 days.

John meets all the criteria for ICP effective December 1, 2007, and is approved for MI T, which provides basic Medicaid coverage. He is ineligible for ICP-related services for 3.7 months. The penalty period would start on December 1, 2007 and run through March 21, 2008.

Implementation Instructions (Transfer of Assets Processes)

For transfers that occur on or after November 1, 2007, apply the new DRA policies. For transfers that occur before November 1, 2007, apply pre DRA policies.

SPECIAL ASSET POLICIES

Annuities

Annuity Disclosure

In order to receive assistance under Medicaid long-term care programs, an applicant/recipient must disclose their ownership interest in **any** annuity. This also applies to a community spouse.

Annuity of an Applicant/Recipient

The purchase of an annuity on or after November 1, 2007 by an individual (or his designated representative) will be evaluated under transfer of asset policies.

Implementation of the DRA Asset Provisions
Page 5

If an annuity meets all of the criteria listed below, it is not considered an asset transferred without fair compensation and is excluded as an asset in the eligibility determination. The periodic payments (including the interest portion) are counted as unearned income in the eligibility determination and patient responsibility.

1. Names the State of Florida (AHCA) as the <u>primary</u> beneficiary, for the total amount of medical assistance paid on behalf of the applicant/recipient, except for when the individual has a spouse, minor or disabled adult child. In this case, the State of Florida may be named as the secondary beneficiary after the spouse, minor or disabled adult child.

   Note: If the spouse or minor/disabled child disposes of their interest in the annuity for less than fair market value (for example, transferred their interest to someone who does not meet the criteria), the State <u>must</u> be named primary beneficiary or the applicant/recipient will be subject to a transfer of asset penalty.

2. Is irrevocable (cannot be cashed in) and non-assignable (cannot be sold or transferred to a third party).

   Note: An annuity that is revocable and/or assignable is not considered a transferred asset, but is a <u>countable</u> asset. If the annuity is revocable, the asset value is the amount the purchaser would receive from the annuity issuer if the annuity is cancelled. If the annuity is assignable, the asset value is the amount the annuity can be sold for on the secondary market.

3. Makes payments (that include both principle and interest) to the individual in equal amounts during the term of the annuity, with no balloon or deferred payments.

4. Is actuarially sound based on the actuarial tables used by the Social Security Administration. **(Refer to Appendix 14, Program Policy Manual)**

If an annuity does <u>not</u> meet all of the above criteria, the total amount of funds transferred into the annuity is considered a transfer, except for when the annuity is revocable or assignable, then the annuity is countable as indicated in the note under #2 above.

Note: Certain transactions that occur on or after November 1, 2007 make an annuity (including an annuity purchased before November 1, 2007) subject to the above asset transfer policies. Such transactions include changes to the course of the payments or treatment of the income or principal, as well as additions of principal, elective withdrawals, requests to change the distribution, and elections to annuitize the contract.

Implementation of the DRA Asset Provisions
Page 6

Annuities of Community Spouses

The purchase of an annuity on or after November 1, 2007 by the community spouse
will be evaluated under transfer of asset policies with a potential penalty against the
applicant/recipient spouse, unless the annuity meets the following criteria:

1. Names the State of Florida (AHCA) as the primary beneficiary, for the total
   amount of medical assistance paid on behalf of the applicant/recipient spouse,
   except for when the spouse has a minor or disabled adult child. In this case,
   the AHCA shall be named as secondary beneficiary after the minor/disabled
   child; and

2. Is actuarially sound based on the spouse's age on actuarial table used by the
   Social Security Administration (Refer to Appendix 14, *Program Policy
   Manual*).

DRA transfer provisions do not require a community spouse's annuity to be
irrevocable, non-assignable, or pay equal payments that include both interest and
principal. However, the term "transactions" and policy in the "**Note**" on the previous
page (except for elective withdrawals) may also apply to a community spouse's
annuity.

The recipient will be required to report changes that may have occurred to the
community spouse's annuity (for example, change in beneficiary designation) that
could result in the annuity being evaluated as a transfer of assets. However,
annuities purchased by the community spouse after approval of long-term care
Medicaid for the recipient spouse are not evaluated for transfer of assets policies.

Annuities Not Considered Under Transfer Provisions

Individual Retirement Accounts (IRAs) or annuities established by an employer or
employee are not considered under the transfer of assets policies. These include
Individual Retirement Annuities, Simplified Employee Pensions and Roth IRA's.

Annuities (or accounts) discussed in this section are considered under retirement
fund policies as found in manual passage 1640.0505.04.

Evaluating Annuities

When an individual applying for or receiving Medicaid long-term care programs
indicates ownership interest in an annuity, use the following procedures:

- Request a complete copy of the annuity contract.
- Use the Evaluating Annuities' job aide (Attachment 1), to help determine if the
  annuity can be excluded from the transfer of asset policies.

Implementation of the DRA Asset Provisions
Page 7

- Send CF-ES 2355, *Letter to Annuity Issuer*, (**Attachment 2**) to the annuity issuer when the State is named beneficiary of the annuity. Attach a copy of the annuity to the form.

- At the annual review, if the recipient has indicated a change has occurred in the annuity, send Form CF-ES 2355 to the issuer.

- When an issuer reports changes to a recipients' or spouse's annuity, evaluate the effect of the change for potential asset transfer penalty.

Notifying AHCA

Use Form CF-ES 2356, *Third Party Recovery Transmittal*, (**Attachment 3**), to notify AHCA of each annuity naming the Agency as beneficiary. Attach a copy of the annuity to the transmittal and mail to:

> Health Management Systems, Inc.
> 2002 Old St. Augustine Road, Suite E-42
> *Tallahassee, FL 32301-4887*

The Department must notify AHCA of the death of an individual whose annuity named them as a beneficiary. This will assist them in recovering Medicaid dollars from the annuity.

Implementation Instructions

For annuities purchased on or after November 1, 2007, apply the new DRA policies. For annuities purchased before November 1, 2007 and within the look-back period, apply pre-DRA policies.

Home Equity Exceeding $500,000

Home Equity Policy

Individuals with equity interest in their home in excess of $500,000 are not eligible for long-term care. Individuals may qualify for Medicaid benefits other than nursing facility or other long-term care services.

Home equity is calculated using the current market value of the home minus any debt. The current market value is the amount for which it can reasonably be expected to sell on the open market in its geographic area. If a home is held in any form of shared ownership, consider only the fractional interest of the person requesting long-term care services.

NOTE: Existing policies found in manual passage 1640.0534 regarding the asset value of the homestead have not changed.

Implementation of the DRA Asset Provisions
Page 8

Exceptions to Home Equity Policy

(1) Home equity policy does not apply if any of the following are residing in the individual's home:

- The individual's spouse,
- The individual's child (biological or adopted without regard to the child's marital status) under age 21, or
- The individual's blind or disabled (per SSA) child of any age.

Accept individual's statement for relative(s) relationship and residence in the institutionalized individual's home, unless questionable.

(2) The home equity policy may be waived when denial of long-term care eligibility would result in demonstrated hardship to the individual.

Verifying and Evaluating Home Equity

- Accept the statement of the applicant/recipient or their designated representative regarding how much their property is worth and how much they owe, unless questionable.

- If the equity value is $450,000 or greater, the applicant/recipient or their designated representative must obtain the market value from a knowledgeable source. At this point, request proof of indebtedness against the home.

- If it appears that an individual may have home equity exceeding $500,000, contact the client or their designated representative to confirm that the exception listed under (1) above does not apply.

Implementation Instructions

Evaluate home equity at the point of application and annual review/interim contact for individuals who file an initial application or reapplication for long-term care services on or after November 1, 2007.

Do not apply home equity policy to individuals who file an application for long-term care programs prior to November 1, 2007 and were determined eligible and have had no break in eligibility.

Implementation of the DRA Asset Provisions
Page 9

Continuing Care Retirement Community (CCRC) Entrance Fees

CCRC Entrance Fees policy applies to all **SSI-Related Medicaid** programs.

Definition of a Continuing Care Retirement Community

Continuing Care Retirement Communities, also known as life-care communities, are facilities that provide residents with a range of flexible services that include shelter and health care in return for an entrance fee and periodic monthly payments. Individuals receive specific services and depending on the contract terms and payment plan may shift between independent living, assisted living or a nursing facility as health care needs change.

CCRC Entrance Fee Policy

The entrance fee paid by an individual upon admission into a CCRC is considered a countable asset when all of the following conditions are met:

- The individual has the ability to use the entrance fee or the contract provides that the entrance fee may be used to pay for care when the individual's income and assets are insufficient to pay for their care.

- The individual is eligible for a refund of any remaining entrance fee upon the individual's death or termination of the contract.

- The entrance fee does not confer an ownership interest in the CCRC.

If the individual has the ability to receive a refund of the entrance fee, the amount which could be refunded must be considered as an available asset, regardless of whether a refund is actually received.

Staff must request and review a copy of the CCRC contract. Once the potential for a refund is established, staff may accept a written or verbal statement from the CCRC as to the amount of the potential refund.

If a refund is no longer available, it is not necessary to evaluate whether the individual received fair market value for the funds used to pay the entrance fee. Unless questionable, staff will assume the individual made a good faith payment for the services provided by the CCRC and would not include the entrance fee as an available asset.

Implementation Instructions

Apply the new policies to new applications, or reapplications filed on or after November 1, 2007. Once a CCRC contract has been evaluated, it is not necessary to reevaluate at review.

Implementation of the DRA Asset Provisions
Page 10

Promissory Notes, Loans and Mortgages

All promissory notes, loans and mortgages signed on or after November 1, 2007 will be considered a transfer of assets without fair compensation unless the promissory note, loan or mortgage meets all of the criteria listed below:

- Has a repayment term that is actuarially sound based on Social Security's life expectancy tables found in Appendix A-14; and

- Has payments made in equal amounts during the term of the loan, with no deferral and no balloon payments made; and

- Does not allow debt forgiveness.

When all of the above criteria are <u>not</u> met, for transfer purposes, the asset value of the promissory note, loan or mortgage is the outstanding balance due as of the date of application for long-term care programs.

If all criteria are met, follow manual passage 1640.0561.03.

<u>Implementation Instructions</u>

For promissory notes signed on or after November 1, 2007, apply the new DRA asset policies. For promissory notes signed before November 1, 2007, apply pre DRA policies.

Purchase of Life Estate Interest

A life estate interest purchased in another individual's home on or after November 1, 2007, may be considered a transfer of assets without fair compensation and be subject to a transfer of asset penalty period. If the purchaser has not resided in the home for at least one year after the date of the purchase, staff must consider the full purchase price paid as a transfer without fair compensation regardless of the value of the life estate or the number of months the purchaser resided in the home.

If the purchaser lived in the home for at least one year after purchasing the life estate, staff must:

- Multiply the fair market value of the property at the time the life estate was purchased by the life estate factor to determine the value of the life estate.

- Deduct the value of the life estate from the purchase price using the life estate factor from the tables in Appendix A-17, *Program Policy Manual*, to determine if fair market value was received, then

- If the amount paid exceeds the value of the life estate, the difference between what was paid and the value received is considered a transfer of assets.

Implementation of the DRA Asset Provisions
Page 11

Temporary absences from the home may not affect the applicant's residency, but each situation must be evaluated to determine if the home continued to be the individual's principal place of residency. Such absences include short-term hospital stays and vacations.

Implementation Instructions

For life estates purchased on or after November 1, 2007, apply the new DRA policies. For life estates purchased before November 1, 2007, apply pre DRA policies.

Long-Term Care (LTC) Insurance Partnership Program Policy

This policy applies only to ICP Nursing Home cases. It does not apply to HCBS, PACE, or Hospice programs.

The Florida Legislature approved Florida's participation in a federal initiative to encourage individuals to purchase long-term care insurance policies to cover future long-term care needs. A qualified LTC Insurance Partnership Policy allows for a special asset disregard if the beneficiary applies for Medicaid nursing home care. Individuals who currently own a standard long-term care policy may ask their insurance carrier to convert the policy to the new qualified LTC Insurance Partnership Policy.

Long-Term Care Insurance Asset Disregard

A beneficiary of a long-term care insurance policy certified under standards established by the Office of Insurance Regulation (OIR) as a qualified state LTC Insurance Partnership Policy, will have a portion of their total countable assets disregarded that is equal to the actual amount of LTC insurance benefits paid out by the insurance company for long-term care benefits.

Example: The insurance company paid out $60,000 for benefits for Ms. Brown, a Medicaid ICP applicant. Staff must subtract $60,000 from the individual's total countable assets when determining if the individual's total countable assets are within the Medicaid program limits.

Documentation Requirements

Individuals who state they have a LTC Insurance Partnership Policy must provide the following documentation from the company issuing the policy:

- The policy qualifies as a LTC Partnership Plan policy as defined by OIR.
- The name of the beneficiary and policy number.
- The total insurance benefits paid to or on behalf of the beneficiary as of the date the documentation is provided.
- The amount of any remaining benefits available.

Implementation of the DRA Asset Provisions
Page 12

Staff may accept the approved Office of Insurance Regulation Form OIR-B2-1781 form (**Attachment 4**) or a similar form developed by the company that provides comparable information.

Documentation is necessary only at application. Follow-up at annual review is necessary only if the individual expects to receive direct payment of benefits beyond the first annual review.

Once approved, if the individual continues to receive LTC insurance benefits directly, follow instructions in manual passage **1840.1007**.

Implementation Instructions

Apply the new DRA polices regarding LTC Insurance Partnership Program Policies to new applications, or reapplications filed on or after November 1, 2007. The asset exclusion will apply for the duration of the individual's Medicaid coverage.

UNDUE HARDSHIP PROVISION

The following hardship provisions apply to transfers, trusts and home equity interest exceeding $500,000.

Undue Hardship Requirements

The DRA requires that all affected individuals be offered an opportunity to demonstrate that the imposition of a penalty period, or excess homestead value policy would create an "undue hardship" prior to the disposition of the application.

Nursing home facilities are allowed to apply for an undue hardship waiver on behalf of an individual, with the consent of the applicant/recipient or the designated representative.

Undue Hardship Process

The undue hardship request is part of the transfer rebuttal procedure. When staff determine a transfer without fair compensation has occurred or that an individual has equity interest in their home that exceeds $500,000 use the following procedure:

- Ensure the transfer rebuttal notice (**Attachment 5**) or, if applicable, CF-ES 2354, *Notice of Excess Home Equity Interest*, (**Attachment 7**) is mailed to the client and designated representative. **Note:** FLORIDA will generate the transfer notice from the AAAT screen. However, if using the manual notice, CF-ES 2264, *Notice of Determination of Asset (or Income) Transfer*, include on the notice a direct contact phone number **other than** the Customer Call Center number.

Implementation of the DRA Asset Provisions
Page 13

- When the customer makes contact, use the *Rebuttal/Undue Hardship Questionnaire* (**Attachment 6**) for transfers or the *Waiver of Home Equity Limit Questionnaire* (**Attachment 8**) for home equity to review the case for potential hardship eligibility.

- Request any additional documentation necessary to substantiate the individual's claim.

- The processor must complete entries under "Processor" on pages 1 and 2 of the ES 2357, *Rebuttal/Undue Hardship Evaluation*, (**Attachment 9**). Sign the form in coordination with the unit supervisor, approving a successful rebuttal. Scan all documents and contact the Circuit/Region Program Office.

  If rebuttal is not successful, the processor will continue the development of Part II (Undue Hardship Evaluation) and forward the evaluation form and documentary evidence to the Circuit/Region program specialist for review and signature approving or denying undue hardship. The entire evaluation must be completed within 10 calendar days following the contact from the applicant/recipient, not considering client delay days.

- Complete the case using the FLORIDA instructions attached to this memorandum based on the outcome of the decision regarding rebuttal/undue hardship.

Implementation Instructions

Use the rebuttal/hardship process discussed in this memorandum for any transfer provisions applied on or after November 1, 2007 (regardless of the date of application or the date of transfer) and for evaluations of excessive home equity interest for applications filed on or after November 1, 2007.

Circuit or Region program office staff that have questions or need additional information about the policies discussed in this memorandum may contact Carrie Sheffield by e-mail, or by telephone at SC 292-8002 or (850) 922-8002. If there are questions about FLORIDA instructions, please contact Pat Brennan by email or at SC 291-2307 or (850) 921-2307.

Attachments

INDEX

●●●

Made in the USA
Columbia, SC
23 November 2021

49351542R00109